PRAISE FOR ER

Dating for Dads

"Useful. Honest. Informative.
A must-read for all single dads."
—Leah Klungness, Ph.D., psychologist
and co-author of *The Complete Single Mother*

"Ellie Fisher writes in such a familiar, reassuring tone, you
feel like you're getting advice from your best buddy from
college. Her common-sense suggestions and game plans
make the prospect of single-parent dating seem much more
natural and far less intimidating."
—Hank Herman, author of *Accept My Kid, Please!*
A Dad's Descent into College Application Hell

"Ellie Slott Fisher is a single dad's best friend! *Dating for Dads*
is warm, funny, sensitive and bursting with great advice.
She proves that fatherhood doesn't preclude
having a fabulous dating life."
—Jane Ganahl, author of *Naked on the Page:*
The Misadventures of My Unmarried Midlife

"It's hard to be a single dad who's dating. Trying to be
sensitive and responsive to the feelings and needs of your
children and the woman you're dating (not to mention your
own) is tough territory for a man to navigate. Ellie Slott Fisher
knows that territory inside and out, and has drawn a perfect
map of it in *Dating for Dads*. Her message is clear and
strong…A good man can do both. Read the book and she'll
tell you how—with respect, wit, even sports analogies."
—Robert Mark Alter, author of *Good Husband,*
Great Marriage: Finding the Good Husband…
in the Man You Married.

MOM, THERE'S A MAN IN THE KITCHEN AND HE'S WEARING YOUR ROBE: The Single Mother's Guide to Dating Well Without Parenting Poorly

"In the voice of a trusted girlfriend, Fisher delivers honest advice, a fresh perspective and comic relief as she guides newly single moms toward the goal of dating well without parenting badly."
—*Publishers Weekly*

"This book offers practical advice on balancing dating and parenting and on preparing oneself and one's children for the prospect of dating again and all the possible consequences. . . . Fisher's clear and humorous approach and down-to-earth advice should help maintain healthy relationships among everyone involved."
—*Library Journal,* starred review

"This is real-world, on-the-ground stuff. . . . The blend of dating and parenting is almost seamless in these pages, as in life."
—Knight-Ridder News Service

"[Fisher] combines her own wisdom with anecdotal experience from other moms."
—*Newsday*

"[A] warm-hearted, wonderful book . . . Ellie addresses [issues] with heart, humor and savvy. . . . Ellie's book offers comfort and practical advice from someone who's been there, and made her own inevitable mistakes along the way."
—*Times* (Trenton, NJ)

IT'S EITHER
HER *or* ME

ALSO BY ELLIE SLOTT FISHER

Dating for Dads

Mom, There's a Man in the Kitchen
and He's Wearing Your Robe

IT'S EITHER HER *or* ME

*A Guide to Help a
Mom and Her Daughter-in-Law
Get Along*

ELLIE SLOTT FISHER

BANTAM BOOKS TRADE PAPERBACKS
NEW YORK

A Bantam Books Trade Paperback Original

Copyright © 2010 by Ellie Slott Fisher

Published in the United States by Bantam Books, an imprint of The Random House Publishing Group, a division of Random House, Inc., New York.

BANTAM BOOKS and the rooster colophon are registered trademarks of Random House, Inc.

Library of Congress Cataloging-in-Publication Data
Fisher, Ellie Slott.
It's either her or me : a guide to help a mom and her daughter-in-law get along / Ellie Slott Fisher.
p.   cm.
ISBN 978-0-553-38594-6
1. Mothers-in-law and daughters-in-law.   2. Interpersonal relations.   I. Title.
HQ759.25.F57   2010
646.7'8—dc22   2009048097

Printed in the United States of America

www.bantamdell.com

2 4 6 8 9 7 5 3 1

To my son, Noah

Foreword

by Beatrice S. Lazaroff, Ph.D.

I am a counseling psychologist who has been in private practice for almost thirty years. I am also a daughter, a daughter-in-law, a sister, a sister-in-law, a wife, a mother of two sons, and, I hope, a future mother-in-law to someone who will probably have a mother. I have seen the toll stress takes on people when they are involved in relationships that are problematic, intense, and ones in which it seems the conflicts will never be resolved. I have counseled mothers who dislike their son's girlfriend or wife, daughters-in-law who detest their mother-in-law, and sisters who have tried to sabotage a brother's relationship. But fortunately, I have also observed the kindness and maturity in women—on all sides of the relationship—who successfully negotiate this very tricky terrain and learn to get along out of love for their husband, son, or brother.

To understand the critical need for this book by Ellie Slott Fisher, it is imperative to recognize stress and its effect, and how relationships can create a good deal of it. Stress is the emotional and physical sensation we feel when we are under pressure. This pressure can come not only from relationships but also from illness, work, children, finances, and other aspects of our lives. Centuries ago, when a person became scared over confronting a man-eating beast, he had two choices: flee or fight to the death. With either decision, the stress abated. This is called the General Adaptation Syndrome or fight-or-flight response as identified by noted endocrinologist Dr. Hans Hugo Bruno Selye. Today a young man who faces confrontation between his mother and his significant other is unlikely (and unable) to fight or flee. This inability to find a quick, easy solution builds unresolved stress, which leads to more serious problems. The human body can only tolerate so much. Over time, prolonged and unresolved stress can cause debilitating physical or emotional illnesses. The body's immune system is compromised.

Holmes and Rahe's Life Stress Scale—developed in 1967 and still in use today—attributes stress points to certain life events. Psychiatrists Dr. Thomas Holmes and Dr. Richard Rahe believe that if a person accumulates 300 or more life stress points in one year, he or she will most likely become either physically or emotionally ill. Not surprisingly, among the stresses that appear on their scale, many have some connection to relationships. For example, divorce is assigned 73 stress points, marital separation 65, marriage itself 50, pregnancy 40, the gain of a new family member 39, arguments with a spouse 35, a son or daughter leaving home 29, and trouble with in-laws also 29.

These family-generated stresses help explain how the relationship between the women in a man's life can result in significant stress on all the involved parties. Unlike leaving a stressful job or moving away from noisy neighbors, it's not easy to break up with a family, and usually we have little say as to who can join it. The conflicts are often most evident when the couple plans their wedding. The extent to which all the women get involved, from the mothers to the bride, can result in tension. The bride and her mother might choose to exclude the groom's mother from the arrangements, or the groom's mother may take over completely—financially and otherwise—leaving the bride feeling restricted. In the end, it's common for wedding planning to cause a lot of stress.

But the wedding is only one of the issues that can lead to anxiety in relationships. The combinations and permutations of what conflicts can occur among mothers, sons, wives, sisters, mothers-in-law, and other extended family members are endless. Arguing with a spouse creates stress not only on the couple but also on any family members who are privy to it. Pregnancy and grandchildren, despite bringing happiness, can also give rise to conflict and stress because of petty jealousies and possessiveness.

It is not uncommon for men or women to feel stressed by the relationships they have with their in-laws. The couple may have chosen each other, but they have inherited the other's family members. If anyone fails to get along, the stress is felt by everyone. The husband feels stuck in between two women he loves—or more if there are sisters. His mother stresses because, in her estimation, the girl isn't good enough for her son, and she finds she has to walk on eggshells when they are together. The wife is angry because the husband either caters to his mom or doesn't stand up to her, and the mom is outright nasty. All of this discord stems from inadequate communication, ineffective assertiveness, and often a lack of self-esteem.

The son/husband is the pivotal force in resolving the conflicts. He needs to be self-aware and clear about his wants and then assertively and effectively communicate them to both his wife and his mother. The man who remains passive and intentionally ignorant is being disrespectful to all the parties involved. If the mother or sister or wife also learn direct, assertive, and effective communication, then most issues will be resolved in a decent manner, and the end result will be a reduction in stress.

In *It's Either Her or Me*, Ellie Fisher, as she does in her first two books on relationships, *Mom, There's a Man in the Kitchen and He's Wearing Your Robe,* and *Dating for Dads,* lifts the cover of politeness, secrecy, and phoniness and forces everyone, including herself, to come clean. She admits to having made the same errors in judgment as have the men and women she interviews for her books. As the mother of a son who dates, as a onetime daughter-in-law, and as a woman with a significant other—who also, by the way, has a mom—Fisher understands the complexities of the relationships of all the women in a man's life. Furthermore, because she builds her advice on extensive research and interviews, she has gained even deeper insight into the subject and consequently offers invaluable tips on how to deal with these issues in a compassionate and sometimes humorous manner. Since some level of stress is almost guaranteed when a couple enters a relationship, this new book on the in-law connection should be required reading.

Acknowledgments

In the course of writing this book, I discovered that every woman I met was in some way affected by another woman connected to her son, her spouse, or her brother. Since there is no escaping this dynamic, I was fortunate to have a lot of help in understanding it.

For professional advice I turned to two superb teachers, clinical psychologist Dr. Beatrice Lazaroff and licensed professional counselor Esther Ganz. Not only are they wise and compassionate therapists, but they have experienced firsthand the woman-to-woman dynamic in a guy's life. Both have mothers-in-law, sisters-in-law, brothers-in-law, and sons who have girlfriends.

For legal information, I sought the advice of renowned family practice attorney Cheryl Young and grandparenting expert Amy Goyer, formerly with AARP and currently with Grandparents.com. Both shared their vast knowledge and their experiences so that I could fully comprehend the issues regarding grandparents.

I interviewed dozens of mothers, wives, girlfriends, sisters, husbands, boyfriends, and sons. Their names have been changed, because I recognize that their relationships will continue to develop; like a fine wine, they can improve with age, and I wouldn't want their thoughts on a given day to negatively affect those relationships. A few have given me the honor of thanking them publicly. They include: Allison Levin, Dana DeChristofaro, Lindsey Alexander, Gina D'Amato-Kaufman, Lisa Waldman, Valerie Alexander, Marcie Maloney, Francine Bank, Lynn Connolly, Arden Miller, Ari Bank, Lindsay Friedman, and Joy Bank. I wish that they, and the others who welcomed us into their lives, find a happy and sustained peace among all the women their loved ones love.

I also want to thank my editor, Danielle Perez, who recognized the need for a book that discussed this issue with a positive spin and addressed both the mothers and the sons' significant others. Her brilliant editing and perspective as a daughter-in-law helped me fine-tune this book. And a huge thank-you to my agent, Susan Cohen, who once again found a home for me.

But most of all, I need to recognize the people who made such a book possible: my mother, Thelma Sayare; my late mother-in-law, Dorothy Fisher; my very significant other, Jonathan Roth; my dear Rebecca Lee; my daughter, Debra Fisher, and my son, Noah Fisher.

Contents

Introduction

I have loved all of my son's girlfriends.

As if I had a choice.

As mothers of sons eventually discover, one day you're relegated to the backseat of the car you helped pay for, while some young, nimble thing regally claims the passenger seat. It hits you at that moment: You've been replaced. Now the only way to retain some semblance of your cherished role as most venerated female in your son's life is by getting along with his girlfriend.

As the girlfriend of this guy, you knowingly chose him for the whole package: his unmatched wit, boyish good looks, and genuine compassion. You just never considered the string attached: his mother. Whether she appears on the scene with polite reservations or intimidating enthusiasm, you can be certain of one thing: She isn't about to give up her son without a fight.

There is no relationship on earth quite like the one between a man's mother and his girlfriend/fiancée/wife. These two women connect in a parallel universe where no man has ever gone before. Nor does he want to. In fact, he's often most content to keep his head securely in the clouds, in blissful ignorance of the world-class competition unfurling around him.

This competition will exist even if the relationship between the women is amicable and loving. After all, who gets to host Christmas now? Who really makes the best meat loaf (in his opinion)? Who assumes which role in planning the wedding? It doesn't take much—a misspoken word, a forgotten gift, an insincere thank-you—for this relationship to become troubled or second-guessed.

For the mom, the subtle crumbling of her status as preeminent female in her son's eyes coincides with his discovery of girls. Who *is* this child trading Mickey Mouse soap for men's cologne? When did those hockey posters come down and Scarlett Johansson go up? These changes portend a future in which Mom will struggle to preserve a place in her son's life. It doesn't matter that she sweated through labor, held him until his fever broke, repeatedly spelled *Mississippi* until he got it right, and comforted him when he missed a goal. She now has to learn when it is appropriate to voice an opinion without putting the other female—or her son, for that matter—on the defensive. She has to know how to reach out to her son's new love without being overbearing. And she has to learn that in order for her son to have a healthy relationship with a girlfriend, she has to let them work things out by themselves.

Meanwhile, the girlfriend or wife faces her own set of challenges. Her job is to look good without making the mom—as infuriating as she might be—look bad. If she is disrespectful to or inconsiderate of the mom, it's only a matter of time before the guy thinks his mother is being victimized, and will begin defending her. This is especially true if the mom continues to quietly and cunningly indulge him. (Only *she* knows he likes his sandwiches cut on an angle, and only *she* can keep his undershirts sparkly white. If mom can't, she runs out and buys new ones, and washes them before giving them to him, folded.)

And although most guys won't admit it, they can't help but compare their significant others with their mothers. Not only is that a tall order for a girlfriend or wife to fill, but her work doesn't end there. For her relationship with her man to flourish, she also must learn how to show deference to his mother (firebrand that she is) while simultaneously making sure this *other* woman knows her place.

Further exacerbating these woman-to-woman relationships is the fact that each woman views them from her own perspective. Girlfriends love, respect, and adore this guy but also see his flaws, and may impatiently try to correct them. Mothers, on the other hand, are sometimes loath to acknowledge their precious boy's faults—and when they do, they often dismiss them as endearing.

I realize many moms—me included—may not want to hear this, but if you really value your son's happiness and if he appears to be content with this other woman, you have to relinquish your first-place standing. And smile while doing it.

As a mother of an adorable, perfect, no-girl-good-enough for him (okay, at least I'm honest) twenty-four-year-old son who has had numerous relationships, I know how difficult it is to go from being the light of my little boy's life to being kept completely in the dark. In order to stay connected with my son, I must like his girlfriend. In fact, I just adore my son's current girlfriend, and the one before her, and I'm positive I'll adore the next one. I know this because I love my son. In order for me to remain a part of his life, I will always love his girlfriends.

So how do I do this? How does his girlfriend deal with me? What role does my son have in cultivating this relationship? How do we deal with all the other influences—my daughter, his girlfriend's mom, his girlfriend's sister? To learn how best to foster this woman-to-woman dynamic, I turned to two highly regarded therapists: clinical psychologist Dr. Beatrice Lazaroff, who counsels couples and families in her Main Line Philadelphia practice, and licensed professional counselor Esther Ganz, in private practice in Monmouth County, New Jersey. With more than fifty years of experience between them, they both understand the difficulties inherent in these relationships. They also each happen to have two sons.

To further explore the tricky but potentially rewarding relationship between a guy's mom and his significant other, I also interviewed mothers, girlfriends, wives, sisters, and the conveniently clueless males themselves. All names have been changed to guarantee a pleasant Thanksgiving.

You'll peek into the lives of several moms, including Lily, who admits she has ignored the existence of her son's long-term girlfriend for years in the hope she'll just fade away. She hasn't. There's also Sue, whose vision of her son marrying a sweet, wholesome girl, having cute little grandchildren with their father's nose and mother's eyes, evaporated when he announced he was marrying an older divorced woman with a child. Another mother, Caroline, keeps mum every time her grandchildren visit with dirty mussed-up hair and mismatched clothes, demanding Grandmom become a vegan. But then there is also Nicci who adores her son's girlfriend, a lovely young woman who by the way doesn't get along with her own mother. (Yes, there's a correlation here.)

You'll be introduced to the girlfriends—some who try to befriend their boyfriend's mom, and others who admittedly make her life hell. One of them, Marie, mourns the death of her own mom so intensely that she has no tolerance for her annoying, hippyish mother-in-law. She frequently prohibits her mother-in-law from visiting her grandchildren as a punishment for being, well, just for being. You'll empathize with Kelly, whose boyfriend's mom acts nauseatingly sweet in front of him, then tosses zingers when he's not in the room. And with Hannah, whose love affair with a guy from a culture foreign to her own was deliberately hijacked by his overbearing mother. You'll meet another young wife, Cassie, who complains that her husband visits his mother twice a week but refuses to take her along.

And just when we think the only female-to-female hurdle in a guy's relationship involves his mom and his girlfriend, we'll discover an even bigger challenge: his sister. Sisters, unlike most moms and girlfriends, tend to hold little back. They want to like their brother's girlfriend or wife, really they do, but it's just so hard. Candace can't see how her brother's artsy girlfriend can ever fit in with her conservative family, and Laura bluntly tells her younger brother to stop seeing the girl who started out "very needy, and then turned psycho." Joan tries to get along with the wives of her three brothers because she knows what it feels like to be the target—a position she holds with her husband's own sisters.

It's also particularly difficult for the guy's girlfriend to compete with his sister for the affections of the mother. Janet feels stung by her husband's sisters' jealousy, which is triggered by her close relationship with their mother. They act rude and exclusive, and needle Janet by befriending their other brother's wife. "It doesn't help that I come from a different background and they look down on me," she says. "They wanted their brother to marry another princess like themselves, which is what the other sister-in-law is like. I'm not who they would have chosen for him."

And then there are the guys. Loving, caring, intelligent men. It's not a matter of their burying their heads in the sand—okay, for some it is—it's more a matter of feeling trapped in a no-win quandary. They love all the women in their lives and are easily made to feel guilty if they choose sides. But choosing sides is what they have to do and sometimes at the risk of changing their relationship with the other woman. Adam is one of these men. A good-looking, Ivy League–educated, firstborn child, he can't help but put his mother's needs over his girlfriend's. Like a lot of sons whose mothers are single, Adam feels guilty and, consequently, responsible for his mother's happiness. So when his mother comes to visit, he indulges her by excluding his girlfriend from their plans.

No serious romantic relationship will survive if a guy consistently puts his mother first.

Ironically, although the guys may be reluctant to intervene, they are the ones who can be most effective in improving these female relationships. So when you're finished reading this book, you might want to pass it on to the man in your life—especially since he's the reason you bought it in the first place.

Any woman who has found herself in the mom-girlfriend-wife-sister mix knows the issues are endless: The man defers to *her* all the time. Everyone anguishes over whose holiday dinner to attend. The couple announce they are moving in together and his mom is not invited to help decorate—though *her* mom is. (As I said, there are a lot of woman-to-woman dynamics in this guy's life.) The couple's religions or cultures are so foreign to each other that the mom, girlfriend, sister (you fill in the blank) is devastated, even a little intimidated. Or sometimes this happens: Just as the women become attached—the mother or daughter each never had—the guy informs everyone the romance is over.

When I first told people I was writing a book on the often-times volcanic relationships among the women in a guy's life, some of the moms told me it didn't apply to them. They liked their son's choice. So then I asked them how they got along with their husband's mom or his sisters. "Oh, them. Well, that's different." What I also discovered is that it is rare for a woman not to have some sort of relationship with another female connected to her husband or son. Except for my friend Vickie. She has two daughters, a husband who has no sisters, and a deceased mother-in-law. I thought someone had finally stumped me. But then I asked her, "Do your daughters' boy-friends have moms?"

As women discover when their child enters a serious ro-mance, all the females connected to the couple—mothers, sis-ters, grandmothers, aunts—can impact the relationship. And if someone is influencing your child's relationship, that affects you. My friend Fran, who has two married sons, realizes that even though she gets along with her two daughters-in-law, if they don't get along with each other, their poor relationship will have a negative impact on the entire family.

Whew! The more I thought about this woman-to-woman dynamic, the more I realized it's practically limitless: the girl's mother and the boy's mother (the Yiddish language inge-niously coins a word for this relationship: *mechutonim*), the fa-ther's new wife and the son's girlfriend, the son's mother and his father's new wife, and so on. This really does affect most women in some way. It also touches every culture, and some of those cultures might make the rest of us rethink our some-times petty grievances with our own mother-in-law or daughter-in-law. For instance, the traditional Japanese expect their oldest son and his wife to move into his parents' home and take care of them, *forever*.

Interestingly, this custom has steadily declined since the early 1960s for reasons that have everything to do with how the women get along. Today many Japanese mothers prefer living with their daughters rather than their daughters-in-law. A lot of these older women have less-than-fond memories of their own mothers-in-law, who taught them household chores and then demanded they do them. Now the daughter-in-law often dominates and makes demands of the mother-in-law. The guys, typically, try to stay out of the conflict.

Cultural issues aside, this woman-to-woman dynamic also reaches back through American history, most notably to the legendary strained relationship between Sara Delano Roosevelt and her daughter-in-law, Eleanor. Eleanor was a shy, unworldly twenty-year-old when she married her handsome distant cousin, Franklin Roosevelt, the only child of James and Sara. The mother of the groom refused to hide her displeasure. "[Sara] was strong willed, controlling, opinionated, and inflexible. She does not seem to have been enthusiastic about any of the young women her son courted, and when he fell in love and proposed marriage to Eleanor Roosevelt, she tried to change his mind and insisted that the engagement be kept secret for a year," according to the Eleanor Roosevelt Papers Project sponsored by George Washington University.

Like a lot of moms of sons, Sara was unprepared, and was certainly unwilling, to relinquish her treasured child to another woman. Even after the young couple married in 1905, Sara continued to orchestrate their lives. She built them a townhouse duplex in Manhattan so they could live in one half, and she in the other, and a summer cottage next to her own on the island of Campobello. The book *Eleanor and Franklin* by Joseph P. Lash notes that after Sara's death in 1941, Eleanor wrote to a friend, "It is dreadful to have lived so close to someone for 36 years and feel no deep affection or sense of loss. It is hard on Franklin, however." She went on to say that her mother-in-law's "strongest trait was loyalty to her family . . . She wasn't just sweetness or light, for there was a streak of jealousy and possessiveness in her when her own were concerned."

Sara Delano Roosevelt held no exclusive right to the title of Domineering Mother-in-Law. Such women have been known throughout the ages, finding their way into ancient proverbs: "A mother-in-law made of sugar still tastes bitter," say the Catalonians; "A mother-in-law and daughter-in-law can be cooked together but they can never be tender," add the French. And if you are a mother yourself, you'll nod knowingly at this Arabian proverb: "When you die, your sister's tears will dry as time goes on, your widow's tears will end in another's arms, but your mother will mourn you until the day she dies."

The media, whether it's comedians with their nonstop "Take my mother-in-law, please" jokes or movies or television, has focused and capitalized on the mother-in-law/daughter-in-law relationship more than any other family dynamic. And almost never in a positive light. Long-running, notable television shows such as *Everybody Loves Raymond* showcase this. Imagine *your* mother-in-law not only living across the street from you but walking into your house repeatedly and unannounced. The show *The Jeffersons,* on which George's mom insulted his wife, Weesie, nonstop, drew laughs because it was so true to real life. Movies, too, such as *Monster-in-Law,* entertain by spotlighting the dreary side to this relationship.

And of course, every mother of a boy has heard the adage that is practically embroidered on those powder-blue onesies: "A daughter is your daughter for life; a son is a son until he takes a wife."

Despite these stereotypes, there's no reason why the woman who raised him and the woman who weds him can't have a relationship that enriches everyone. It does not have to dissolve into "It's Either Her or Me." It's not always easy, I realize, but in the next eight chapters you will learn how to improve this dynamic. You will understand that both women are vying for first place, which as hard as it is for a mom to accept this, must be awarded to the girlfriend or wife if she truly makes the son happy. Ultimately, that's what all moms want anyway—their sons to be happy.

Each woman must understand her role. What can a mom ask? "Are you two thinking of marriage?" "You've been married five years, are you planning on having children?" Can you voice an opinion? Can you comment on her being a lousy housekeeper? "You know Joey's allergic to dust, don't you?" Should you let your son confide in you about his love life? Careful, here, I know it's tempting.

And the girlfriend: How do you relate to a woman who thinks she's losing her son? Her thoughts are filled with memories of running to school with his forgotten homework and gym clothes, and providing comfort when he didn't make the team. You've gotten to know—and love—a self-sufficient man who needs no mothering. And how should you refer to her? She wants you to call her Mom but you'd feel more comfortable calling her by her first name. You're sleeping with her son but until you're married, she expects you to stay in separate rooms at her house. You're pleased your boyfriend loves his mother, but how close is too close?

This book will also cover the moms and the girlfriends who are certifiably horrible, the situations that are compounded by differences in religion or age, the other relatives who intervene—especially the boy's father and how his relationship with the girlfriend has bearing on the boy's mother, particularly if the parents are divorced. The relationship between the guy and his wife's dad can also have an impact on the women. If it's adversarial, almost certainly the guy's mom will dislike her daughter-in-law's family.

I'll devote an entire chapter to the sisters, whose relationship with their brother is very different from their mother's. They consider the wife or girlfriend to be a contemporary, which can be a plus if they become friends, or an impairment if they find her unworthy of deferential treatment. She's just a person interfering in their close friendship with their brother. Sisters tend to be more honest, letting everyone know how they really feel about *her*. "Love her. She's great." Or "Hate her. She's evil." As the girlfriend, how do you handle a difficult sister? Is she overprotective of her little brother? Or too in awe of her older one? And how can you get close to your mother-in-law without threatening her *real* daughter? How do you turn his sister into the sister you always wanted?

I'll discuss everyone's role in planning a wedding. How do you include your mother-in-law-to-be? You've envisioned your wedding party elegantly attired in black. She wonders who died. And if you're the groom's mom, do you wait to be asked to go to the tasting, or do you invite yourself along? Can you have input on the wording on the invitation? After all, you're paying for the music and the rehearsal dinner. Before you get involved in any wedding arrangements, you should understand that planning one is taxing on everyone. Yet how everyone defines his or her role leading up to this special day may have a lifelong impact on how the women will get along once they're family.

All of this leads you to the endgame: grandkids, the wife's ultimate clout. As the mother of the guy, how do you handle your role of grandmom without being meddlesome or judgmental? Don't lose sight of your goal, which is to spend time with your grandchildren. And as the daughter-in-law, you may not realize it just yet, but you will want your kids to love their grandmother. So it behooves you to set some fair and reasonable child-rearing guidelines for everyone to follow.

Although I realize that this woman-to-woman dynamic can be difficult, it can, and should, be wonderful, adding a rich dimension to the lives of everyone involved. Having been married to someone's son, as well as having raised one, I know without question that this can be the case. I loved my husband's mother and never understood all the jokes about manipulative mothers-in-law. I assumed I was just lucky. Then two years after she passed away and my own son entered a serious relationship, I finally understood how my mother-in-law ensured she and I would get along.

She knew when to bite her tongue.

Consequently, she maintained a wonderful relationship with her only son, and an even better one with me. She wisely understood that if a mother wishes to remain involved in her son's life as he moves from childhood into adulthood, she must welcome his girlfriend with open arms.

It's double or nothing.

———

Oh, and by the way, I promised my son and his current girl-friend that this book will not cover their relationship—only his previous ones. While this may sound extremely considerate on my part, it's really about self-preservation.

I can't wait to babysit my future grandkids.

IT'S EITHER
HER *or* ME

_____

CHAPTER ONE

Moms and Girlfriends
Vie for First

For most moms, it comes about quite unexpectedly. All of a sudden the little boy who refused to part with his well-worn *Toy Story* pajamas, despite the fact that Buzz Lightyear's face had faded to obscurity, is wearing aftershave. And he doesn't even shave. That child who shrieked "Mommy! Mommy! Mommy!" when you returned home from work now grunts "Uh-huh" and "Nah" in response to your questions. Yet you overhear him speaking animatedly and loquaciously to someone on his cell phone.

This new, redesigned little boy has moments of unexplained extreme pleasantness, offering to take out the trash before you even ask. (Don't get too excited; these moments are fleeting.) You attribute these changes to his entering puberty with its typical hormonal shifts and turns. While this certainly is true, what's also happening is that your son has embarked on a journey to find a new—and different—love of his life.

Oh sure, you'll still get the requests for money (you may actually recall with fondness his five-dollar allowance) or for help, but that pedestal you've been on for the past fourteen years or so is starting to crack. Now that your son has discovered girls—not just in a stealing-their-lunch-on-the-school-bus way, but as potential intimates—your relationship with him will change.

Meanwhile, as the girlfriend, you hadn't considered how his mother could affect your relationship. You've fallen for a guy who may act one way when he's with you, and another way—not all that pleasingly—when he is with his mom. You'll find yourself treading carefully around this woman, knowing that regardless of what happens between you and your boyfriend, *she* will always love him.

> *It is rare that one can see in a little boy the promise of a*
> *man, but one can almost always see in a little girl the threat*
> *of a woman.*
> —Alexandre Dumas

Who's on First?

A natural order follows the birth of a son. A mother smiles knowingly when his first word is *Dada* and not *Mama*, because, as everyone knows, it's an easier word to form. She directs the barber to cut his hair so he'll mimic an adorable GapKids model when she dresses him for Easter. She arranges his plans for the summer, artfully working them around the family vacation. She anxiously gets him ready for his first school dance, straightens his tie, and takes a picture.

And then she moves over.

As difficult as it is for a mom to step off first base, in order for her to raise an emotionally healthy son who will enter an emotionally healthy adult relationship, she has to be willing to hit a sacrifice fly.

Most moms understand this, but that doesn't make it any easier.

Hope, whose married son recently became a parent, says that as much as she has been reluctant to share her only child with another woman, whom she likes, she recognizes that in order to keep her son in her life, she has to allow his wife to take her place. "If you're going to fight that, you're going to cause friction," Hope says. "I'd never want to do that."

Caroline, another mom with a married son, believes she has been replaced by her new daughter-in-law. "He would talk to me, rather than her, before he got engaged. I do feel replaced," she says, adding with a little resignation, "but I should be. That doesn't bother me."

Family counselor Esther Ganz applauds the way these two moms handle their relationships with their adult sons. As much as a mom might want to maintain some control over her son, and maybe even his significant other, she really only has control over her own feelings. "I would work on myself. It's not the girlfriend's problem. It's mine," Ganz suggests.

For you moms, this may require taking stock of your own life. Has it become too centered on your kids, and not on yourself? Did you give up a career or hobby or other passion once you became a mom? Have you been living vicariously through your kids so that you fear feeling lost when they no longer need you? (A cautionary note to mothers of younger sons: They always will need you, especially when you're ready to retire, play golf, and focus on yourself.) As mothers, you chart your children's development along with your own aging, so the more independent they become, the more ancient you feel. Yet you are really never too old to add a new dimension to your life. You can still get a new job, develop a hobby, go back to school, take a cooking class, learn yoga, travel with your husband or friends. You can make yourself whole. The interesting consequence to all of this is that your sons will be so proud of you—and not feel smothered by your myopic attention to them—that they may even initiate an occasional phone call.

I used to play tennis with a very wise mother of two boys who were a few years older than my kids. When I told her how sad it made me to think of my first child going off to college, especially since I projected a lonely future as a single mom, she reminded me about the universal goal of mothers. That goal is to raise children to be independent, financially and emotionally, so they can develop their own productive lives. It's why you gave them piano lessons, made them go to Sunday school, and insisted they brush their teeth. And those lives should, in the best of circumstances, include falling in love with your replacement.

Amy gets this. She has a thirty-year-old son who just got married. As close as she has always been with him, she claims she doesn't feel less important now that he has a wife. "I really don't. I feel that this is our goal as parents to see our kids become independent, find a loving spouse, replicate what our parents had." She adds, laughing, "I think my husband feels he's being replaced more than I do. When our son got married, my husband acted so depressed, like we were sending him to the gallows rather than to a wife!" Her husband insists, of course, that he has no personal take on this.

You should emulate these three women by being content to move over and give your son's new flame your space, as in a chess game—a kind of queen for a queen, where, if you refuse to budge, you'll end up in a stalemate. I know you understand all of this without my telling you. But deep down inside, it's okay to feel a little saddened by this change.

When the boy's mom readies herself to relinquish her first-place position to the girlfriend, if you are that girlfriend, you have your own set of responsibilities. Coming first in a guy's life comes with a price. Dethroning this other woman (indulge me as I continue the queen metaphor) doesn't mean you get to relegate the Queen Mother to the servants' quarters. No one will tolerate that. And you'll be unfairly viewed as the wicked, heartless daughter-in-law whose husband, by the way, will probably continue speaking to his mother behind your back. Since first place is yours for the taking, try to be magnanimous to the woman you bested. Hopefully, you'll even grow to like her.

Twenty-six-year-old Kelly is trying. Even though she doesn't particularly like her boyfriend's mom, she genuinely feels sorry for her, believing her insecure behavior is in some way the result of her son's own insensitivity. Kelly's boyfriend frequently gets so caught up in his activities that he forgets to call his mom. Because Kelly speaks to her own mother every day, she understands how lonely her boyfriend's mom must feel. Purely out of a sense of obligation—and not out of fondness—she encourages him to call his mother.

As a girlfriend or wife, your being considerate of his mom—giving your regards when her son calls her, offering to let her sit in the front seat of the car with her son (she should refuse but will appreciate that you asked), thanking her when she gives you that perfume that smells a little like Bubblicious—may not only improve your relationship with her but also stabilize her relationship with her son, which will, consequently, effectively strengthen your relationship with him.

And as the boy's mom, you should recognize how difficult it is for the wife or girlfriend to fit in with your family. She tries to be on her best behavior but she feels ill at ease with your daughter, who acts possessively toward her brother, and with your sister, Aunt Jean, who relishes every opportunity to criticize, and with your elderly father, who resents her different religion. Just like the girlfriend, you, too, should offer to take the backseat—figuratively and literally.

One more word on the subject of gifts. My mother-in-law

looked forward to giving me an Estée Lauder gift box every Christmas. I loved the gift the first year, but then by the seventh or eighth Christmas I had stockpiled so much makeup, I could have worn a different shade of lipstick every single day. I never had the heart to tell her I no longer wanted it. She also used to fill her candy dish with pastel-colored mint candies. Being polite, I once told her I liked them. I didn't, but they turned up enclosed with my birthday present and Christmas present every year that followed. Today, four years after my mother-in-law has passed away, I've actually run out of makeup, and I've found myself searching store after store for those tasteless mints.

There will certainly be times that, despite the efforts of the mom and the girlfriend, the guy will do something to hamper their relationship, sometimes unintentionally. Jill, the mother of a twenty-four-year-old son, says her son's girlfriend expects to be with him constantly. But when he needed to buy a suit for a job interview, he asked his mom, rather than his girlfriend, to accompany him. "She got angry because I went instead of her," Jill says. "They fought for a week. She told him, 'I can't believe you took your mother instead of me.'" Now not only is her son feuding with his girlfriend, but the two women are at odds. This incident also emblematizes a dangerous crossing of boundaries in that the boy told his mother about the argument with his girlfriend. There's only one reason for a guy to divulge this: He's unsure of his feelings for his girlfriend, and he wants feedback. Even if he and his girlfriend easily move on from this disagreement, it won't be readily forgotten by the mother, who will subconsciously store it away for the day she is inclined to list all the things wrong with this younger woman. And if the girlfriend learns that he confided in his mother rather than resolving matters privately between them, she will be angry and hurt, and rightly so.

Also significant is that this occasion involves a noteworthy event in this young man's life. He has graduated from college and wants to make a grown-up impression on a prospective employer. His choice to help him pick out this new suit reveals how he views his relationship. If he chooses his significant other over his mother, then he is already comfortable transferring some of the trust he has in his mom to his girlfriend. If he selects his mother over his girlfriend—and she's not offering to pay—then either he feels bad leaving Mom out because she's already upset over his leaving home for good, or he just doesn't feel all that serious with this particular girl.

A girlfriend should not have to fight to be number one in a guy's life; she's entitled to it. If the guy cannot see this, if he continues to seek out his mom's voice rather than his significant other's, then he's not looking to be in a mature, committed relationship. Not only do his actions correlate with how he views his relationships—*Is he ready to pull away from his mom? Does this girlfriend figure prominently in his future plans?* —but they can create a competition between the two women.

Malcolm in the Middle

It's ironic, then, that it's often the guy who complains about feeling stuck in the untenable middle position. Rather than deal with the personality conflicts, unless he witnesses mutual enmity between the two women, he'll just gladly imagine that they're getting along. It's not that these guys don't care enough to get involved; it's that they care too much—for both women.

"Life for the son is hell if the two women don't get along. Unfairly, that's the person who pays the price," says Sue, a mom of a newly married son.

According to clinical psychologist Dr. Beatrice Lazaroff, this role of middleman is inevitable. "Eventually some issue, some comment, some situation will come up and he will get a certain amount of feedback from the girlfriend and the mother. He will feel divided loyalties and will have to negotiate that terrain somehow," she says. "The guy yeses everybody to death, and what happens is that the other people end up getting mad at him because they think he agrees with them, and then he doesn't follow through."

There is a simple explanation for why these guys fail to follow through. They can't win. If, for example, the mother is annoyed with the girlfriend for avoiding her at a family christening, she'll complain to her son. Her son knows that if he relays this to his girlfriend, he'll find himself between two fuming women. All guys get this, and since most men would rather wrestle a hungry bear in the woods in a blinding blizzard than get between two females, can we women really blame them?

Sure we can. Because not only should they take some responsibility, but they also hold all the cards. They know both women will forgive them if they occasionally make a poor decision. In fact, we'll probably transfer the blame to *her* because we don't really want to denounce our son or our boyfriend.

Thirty-five-year-old Paul is one man who understands instinctively that eventually he may have to choose sides. Sensitive and compassionate and with a self-proclaimed strong feminine side, Paul finds any form of confrontation to be offensive. When he fell in love at first sight with his co-worker, Jess, he immediately called his mother. The two women met, enthusiastically greeting each other with a warm hug and a kiss. But the lovefest collapsed a few weeks later when Paul announced his engagement. His mother implored him to wait, insisting they barely knew each other.

"Jess was emotional and dramatic and very upset when I told her what my mother said," Paul recalls. "She told me to stop listening to other people. 'We don't need more time. We know what we're doing.' I felt like I was between a rock and a hard place. On one hand, Mom is giving me advice to hold off the wedding, and the woman I'm about to marry is giving me a calendar date. I wanted to make two people happy."

So Paul went to his "therapist," actually his hairdresser, for advice. "She told me she was in a similar situation. She said to me, 'My husband is very close to his mother. One time he put her before me. I told him that as much as you love and respect your mother, you're starting a new family. You always put your wife first, no matter what.' And hearing that, I made a change on the spot. I came home—my hair looked great—and I had a completely different outlook on how to approach the situation."

From that point forth, Paul opted to support Jess's wishes over his mother's, and although that decision greatly disappointed his mom, it did ultimately work in her favor. When a few issues regarding the wedding arose, Jess felt so secure in her relationship with Paul that she willingly acquiesced to his mom's requests. As for Paul, although he continues to feel like a beleaguered mediator when he has to make a decision between the two women he loves most in the world, he no longer agonizes over whom to choose: It's always his wife.

Not all men catch on as quickly as Paul. They either aren't aware that their mom or significant other is unhappy or they choose not to recognize it. Lazaroff says, "Men do not pick up on clues, nuances, how people seem to feel, attitudes, or moods very well. Women, on the other hand, seem to have a radar about things. They can tell if someone is unhappy, upset, uncomfortable, or controlling." In fact, a guy may fail to notice all that's happening around him. His girlfriend may tell him that his mom ignores her when he's not around and then fawns over her when he is, or he may be so manipulated by the girlfriend's subtle criticism of his mom that he actually starts to question his mother's actions.

Lazaroff says this gender-based state of ignorance is carried through to the boy's dad, who will develop his own opinion about the son's girlfriend—and it may very likely differ from the mother's. It goes back to that parallel universe I talked about earlier. Women relate woman-to-woman. How many times have you told your husband or significant other that your feelings were hurt by a friend who canceled a dinner with you? And your husband says, "She's probably just busy." But you know, boy do you know, that she's still sore about your celebrating your birthday with another friend. So now when you want your husband to recognize the concerns you have about your son's new girlfriend, he's unresponsive. Besides, oftentimes in his mind there are no problems so long as the girlfriend meets his one criterion: She's pretty.

"A dad will not get the same feelings about the son's girlfriend that a mother will," Lazaroff explains. "By the same token, the son may not pick up on the mom or the girlfriend being controlling, et cetera." And as far as being pretty, women know that *pretty* is only skin deep.

Robert, a twenty-nine-year-old who is engaged to be married and the son of a single mom, refuses to come between his mom and his fiancée. They do seem to like each other, and according to Robert, his fiancée tries very hard to earn his mother's respect. "They have a good relationship but to get to a point of feeling like family, I really want them to work it out themselves."

Like I said, a bear in the woods is no match.

Guy's Rule of Thumb: Girlfriend First

When twenty-eight-year-old Adam graduated from college and moved to the East Coast from the Midwest, his girlfriend, Allie, joined him. Although they had been together several years and were committed to each other, Adam neglected Allie whenever his mom visited from out of town. "It was only fair that my mom preferred some time alone with her son, whom she rarely saw," Adam explains. Fortunately for Adam, his girlfriend complied—at least until her job forced her to move away, too.

Then, coincidentally, Allie and his mom picked the same week to take off from work and fly out to visit Adam. Even though Allie had made her plans well in advance of his mom's, Adam told her he didn't want to deal with potential conflicts if they were both there at the same time. "Allie would want to see me. My mom would want to see me," Adam says. "So in the end, I left Allie to deduce that she shouldn't come."

This is not the way to be in a relationship.

If a guy is going to choose his mom over his girlfriend, or refuse to weather their possible differences by not bringing them together, then his relationship with the girl will suffer, if not end. Remember, I'm the mom of a boy I adore, whom I've raised alone since he was five, whom I've driven six hours to hockey tournaments in the early-morning darkness, whose school I snuck into to tell him that he had been accepted into his first-choice college. (The oversized envelope was unglued!) So yes, this is painful for me, too. But Allie should never have been excluded, and Adam's mother was wrong in expecting to be alone with her son and in not insisting that either she would change her plans or they would all be together.

After being scuttled to the side one too many times, Allie finally told Adam she could no longer remain in second place. "I don't disagree with anything she says," Adam admits. "If my mom comes to visit, I always push Allie to the backseat. I think that the aim to please is in my soul but the larger issue is that maybe it means I'm not there yet."

Adam's right. If a guy can't put his girlfriend first, then he's not ready to commit to this particular woman. And maybe it means he never will be.

Dr. Lazaroff says that once a man intends to marry or seriously commit to his girlfriend, he has to consider her needs before his mother's. "That person has to become the primary person in your life," she tells men. "You're not going to be married to your mom. A man who puts his mother before his wife—that will never work."

This thinking applies to the fiancée and her parents as well. According to Lazaroff, a woman who remains overinvolved with her parents will most likely face problems in her marriage. "Often I see this in people who are just immature and don't really get it," Lazaroff says. "Over time the husbands, who have been holding in a slow burn, a slow rage, sometimes act out. They have affairs, or leave, and the woman wonders why. They thought it was going fine." A young mother I know always speaks to her father first, rather than her husband, whether it's to fix a leaky toilet or to get advice on a career move. Apparently, she's either unaware—or just doesn't care—how emasculating this is to her husband. Putting your spouse first is unequivocal whether you're the husband or the wife.

Paul says that ever since he took his hairdresser's advice, he has found it easier to deal with Jess and his mother. Until then, he had been extremely close to his mom, often telling her about concerns or disagreements that arose out of his relationship with Jess. "There's a little more distance now between me and my mother since I've gotten married, but I think that's normal. My mother used to say one thing, and Jess something else. I told my mom there will be cases where I will disagree with you and Jess will be number one. I have to put her before anybody else. Mom was understanding but more quiet than she typically is."

Today Paul says he doesn't think he'll ever again feel ensnared in the middle between the two women he loves most. "I think that's because I made it abundantly clear to my mom that no matter how much it hurts me to upset her, Jess is my wife and she always is going to be first."

Now that I've argued that the girlfriend should come first, I recognize there may be situations in which she shouldn't. In fact, she may be really out of line. As counselor Ganz says, "If she has a personality disorder or is a very difficult person who tries to isolate a guy from his family, then if he puts her first, he's going to lose his family. A lot of this is based on his taking a look at himself to see why he's choosing to be in this relationship. If he doesn't challenge her or her behavior, he's not going to end up a happy person."

Let's look at the broader picture: If a girl really cares about a guy, would she want him to be isolated from his family? Once she feels confident that she takes precedence, she must be willing to accept the other people in his life.

> *It takes one woman twenty years to make a man of her son—*
> *and another woman twenty minutes to make a fool of him.*
> —Helen Rowland, journalist and humorist

Happiness Is a Warm Son

Mothers look for two main criteria in a son's girlfriend: *Does she make him happy? Does she cherish him?* She can cook like Rachael Ray, look like Jessica Alba, and think like Lisa Ling, but if she doesn't put a smile on his face, or if she goes out with her girlfriends when he's home with a fever, she may as well not even try.

Cindy got a call from her married thirty-eight-year-old son asking her to drive him to the hospital for outpatient shoulder surgery. When they returned home from the hospital, her son lay down on the sofa in obvious discomfort. A little while later, his wife came home from work. Cindy says, "She not only didn't acknowledge me, but she didn't acknowledge him and what he had just gone through. She only complained about being tired. I was mad at her for that." If her son was, too, he didn't let on in front of his mother. Instead he merely asked his wife about her day. "I expect her to be the kind of wife I was. She isn't," Cindy says. "My kid, however, chose this woman. Would I have picked her for my son? No. But she does make him happy."

According to Dr. Lazaroff, the barometer of a son's happiness determines how a mother views his relationship with his girlfriend or wife. "Does he seem happy?" Lazaroff says. "Is his life enriched by this person? Does this person care for him, nurture him? Does she support him in things? Can they communicate? If there are parenting issues, can they work it out together? Can they be a team to make their life work out in the future? They want to feel their son or their brother, in the case of a sister, will be happy and will be taken care of. In an odd way, they won't have to keep doing for him—not that they wouldn't want to, but they are glad someone else will, too."

If a guy needs help—maybe he has to go to an emergency room because the doctor's office is closed, or he lost his job and is struggling to find a new one, or he got involved in a fender bender on the way to work—a mother should be prepared for the girlfriend or wife to take charge. In fact, his significant other must be there for him. Because if she isn't, his mother will never forget this failure to help her son, even if it's years later when it happens again.

There are three perspectives to this. There's the mom who would do anything for her son, and if she's willing to surrender him to another woman, she expects that woman to sacrifice all for him, too. There's the girlfriend or wife who sees the mom as overprotective of a man who is very capable of handling, say, filling out job applications on his own. And then there's the guy, who knows that even when he complains about being stuck in between the two females, he's got it made. If the girlfriend doesn't cater to him, he'll simply turn to Mom.

This situation can be exasperating for the girlfriend and, if it's habitual, harmful to the relationship between her and the guy. When April's son and his fiancée moved into an apartment together, the fiancée called her father and asked him to come over to help paint it. Her anguished son then, in turn, called his mom. "Help," he said. "They're getting paint on the drapes, the carpet, everywhere." Distressed for her son and outraged at his fiancée for bringing in her dad, April went over to help him deal with the situation. But as she stood in their living room, arguing with the girl's father, it struck her as absurd to have been thrust into the center of this young couple's relationship. So she backed away and told her son he needed to work through this himself. Good for April. By removing herself, she set clear boundaries for her son, who then, in turn, had to encourage his girlfriend to establish them with her dad.

My mother-in-law would say to me that her son—her only child—treated me like royalty. At first, I resented what I considered a derogatory comment, but then I realized it was because our relationship was so different from the one she had with her husband. My husband, Charlie, and I catered to each other. We also never discussed any of our disagreements with our parents. My parents were unhappy initially when we got married because of our difference in religion, so I knew any dispute—no matter how minor—would be blown out of proportion. Consequently, I never gave them any cause to dislike him, and by clearly showing both sets of parents how happy we were together, we each ended up having wonderful relationships with our in-laws.

Amy thinks her son yields to his wife much too often, but concludes that on the most important issues he stands his ground. "I think with a lot of things she does get her way. But it's not for me to say what their priorities should be. And it's improved. In the beginning, he was more submissive to her wants, but he does seem to be more true to himself now."

Jill's son, on the other hand, is most content when he is not with his girlfriend. "The change in his personality is huge when he's not in communication with her." "He's happy," Jill says. "When he's with her, it's just too hard. I tell him that relationships do not have to be hard when you're in the right one."

Any mother who witnesses her son's contentedness in a relationship will ultimately learn to love that other woman regardless of what she may have thought of her initially. As Hope says: "My feeling is, it's not my place to like her. If she's going to make him happy, that's what matters." Or to butcher a classic Beatles song, "Happiness is, indeed, a warm son."

Single Mamma's Boy

I remember the night before my parents drove me to college for the first time. My packed suitcases were piled up on my bed, and I was sitting on the floor polishing my nails when my mom walked in. She had a small towel in her hand and, with her back to me, she began dusting my already spotless dresser. When she got to my desk chair, she sat down, lowered her head in her hands, and began to cry.

"Yikes, Mom, I'm only going away to school. I'll be home in a few weeks," I said as I stood up and walked over to her, caught between feeling bad and thinking it was funny. She didn't act this way when my older sister left. But then she still had a kid at home.

A month later when I returned home for fall break, I expected my mom to be thrilled to see me—she was—and saddened when I left—she wasn't. Somehow in the short time I was away from home, my parents had adjusted quite nicely to their empty nest and newfound freedom. And why not? They no longer had to nag their children to take out the trash or clean their rooms. And their marriage became even stronger.

Single moms get deprived of this.

We send off our children and return to a nest that isn't just empty, it's cavernous and still. How we suddenly crave those days when we yelled at them to turn down the music, or angrily waded though dozens of crumpled clothes strewn about their floor, or complained about having to make dinner when a yogurt would have been enough for us. And even if we have a new love interest, we no longer have the father of our child with whom to enter this next life phase.

It's also not easy for the children of these single mothers. Guilt and a sense of obligation can result in either being too wrapped up in their mother's life at their own expense or a need to shut her out entirely because to do otherwise paralyzes them from moving forward. Either way, it is difficult for the mother and the son, as well as for the woman who now enters his life.

I know that my reaction to my son's girlfriends is affected by the fact that I am a single mom. My husband died when my son was only five. So conscious am I of my role as sole parent that I worry my being too close to my son could make him seem like a mamma's boy. I go out of my way to give him space. If his father were alive, I would be viewed differently. In fact, if I fretted about him, his dad would probably think it was "cute how she can't let go." But single moms must deliberately cut the apron strings.

And if we don't, we may find ourselves having a poor relationship not only with our son's significant other, but also with him. A young female journalist I know is engaged to a guy whose parents divorced when he was young and whose mother remains single. According to her, this mom became so dependent on her son after the divorce that when she went on dates, she took him along for support. He grew so tired of being responsible for his mother's comfort that once he became engaged, he stopped all communication with her. My friend urges him to call her, but he refuses, saying he is finished with that supporting role.

Marie remembers when she first met her husband's single mom. She had a pierced nose, short skirt, and bare midriff—the mom, not Marie. "I thought she was neat; kind of hippyish, kind of crunchy. She was nice and cordial and wanted to be friends." At first, Marie liked the contrast with her own mom, whom she describes as "old school, ruler of the roost, and not particularly hip." Marie continues, "We started off pretty well. That is, until she began making comments that made me question things. Like she said 'I want to be a good mother-in-law because my mother-in-law ruined my marriage.' Then when my mother died suddenly, things went downhill."

The loss of Marie's mother intensified the resentment and lack of patience she felt toward her husband's mom. Also, at that time her mother-in-law's veneer of politeness began to slip away and she started to blame Marie for every disagreement she had with her son. Although Marie's husband has always defended his wife, he feels guilty hurting his mother. He insists that his mother join them on the holidays even when they are spent at the home of Marie's sister. Marie says, "He tells me, 'She's my mom. I can't leave her alone.' I get it. That's all he has. He's completely estranged from his biological father's family. He doesn't have a choice but to be close to his mother." She adds with a laugh, "But I'm looking for her third husband because when she has a man, she stays out of our lives!"

A lot of girlfriends or wives who have a strong relationship with their own mothers may grudgingly appreciate their boyfriend's mother's situation. Kelly, who adores her own mom, feels sorry for her boyfriend's mother because she is single and spends a lot of time alone. Kelly goes out of her way to be friendly and respectful. His mother, though, rarely affords Kelly the same treatment. "She always gets mad when he comes home and I'm with him. She prefers that he come by himself." Kelly believes that if his mother were happier, especially if she were in a serious relationship herself, she'd be more accepting of her son having a girlfriend.

Most girlfriends and wives whose significant other has a

single mom feel this way. Lazaroff says, "The son's girlfriend would love if the boy's mom had a boyfriend because that would give the mom something or someone else to focus on other than her son and his girlfriend. The girl probably wants the boy all to herself and wouldn't mind a little less scrutiny from his mom. Also, the boy might give the girlfriend more attention then. It's the age-old story about two women competing for one man, even if it's done subconsciously. Both of them don't want to lose any ground or attention from the son/boyfriend."

Ironically, sometimes the son feels torn over his mother having a romantic relationship of her own. Kelly's boyfriend, for instance, says he'd prefer that his mother were involved with someone so she would be happier. However, he admits that he didn't like her last boyfriend.

"The boy could feel threatened by the mom dating for a lot of reasons: He doesn't like the guy, he's overprotective of the mom, or he doesn't want to lose his role as man of the house," Lazaroff explains. "In addition, there could still be feelings left about Mom being widowed or divorced that might be painful to the young man. Maybe he thinks that Mom will fight with the man or will be hurt by him, and it would be safer if she just doesn't date. There's also the whole blended-family fear, and a son's resistance in dealing with another guy. It is just easier if he doesn't have to share Mom with anyone. The dating would threaten his security as both the man of the house and Mom's favorite."

Funny, that's how moms feel when their sons start dating.

Hope knows her son wants her to be involved romantically, but that hasn't stopped him from treating her long-term boyfriend poorly. "Because of my divorce, my son feels he is my protector. He had to assume the role of taking care of me." When Hope started dating a co-worker, her son wasn't pleased. "Maybe he thought I'd be on my own and he'd take care of me.

He acts like he's the man of the house. When we go out with him and his girlfriend, he orders the wine. But when the check comes, he isn't the man anymore. He sits back and lets us pick up the check!"

Hope's son is actually less accepting of her social life then she is of his. "I know he was very upset when I separated from his dad. He didn't want us to be divorced. Then he would have liked me to date a doctor or attorney, which I didn't. I never put that sort of pressure on him. I've allowed him to pick and choose in his own life. In fact, I wanted my kids to go away to school, to experience being on their own to meet people. I'm somewhat more enlightened. It doesn't upset me that he's married and creating a new life—even though, now that he's married, we're not as close. The only thing I didn't want him to do was get married young and make the mistakes I did."

Like Hope's son, Adam not only empathizes with his single mother but also feels somewhat responsible for her well-being. "I am very scared for her now. She is very alone. She doesn't have the friends she thought she would have at this age. I feel a sense of obligation to provide some sort of happiness for her or help her in trying to attain it. I know it's not my responsibility, but at the same time I can only imagine what it's like to be a woman in your fifties and alone."

As one of those women myself, I can honestly say that having a fulfilling, exciting life has little to do with our marital status and more to do with our self-esteem. And no mother, married, divorced, widowed, or single, should ever allow her children to feel responsible for her happiness. They can't be. Only we can. It doesn't really matter how satisfied a mother is in a relationship with either a new husband or a boyfriend, she—as the saying goes—is only going to be as happy as her least happy child. If your child sacrifices his own life—in any way—he isn't going to be happy.

And that will make all the women in his life miserable.

On the Positive Side

We've touched on a lot of the ways the relationship between a guy's mother and his significant other is inherently tense—but we should also consider how this relationship has its fundamental pluses.

For one thing, while a relationship between a mother-in-law and daughter-in-law doesn't have the love-is-blind quality of a blood relationship, it also doesn't have the baggage. If my daughter goes out with a good-looking, successful, and pompous guy she meets at a club, I cringe remembering the last such guy she dated, and how angry she was when he texted her at midnight, days after she expected to hear from him. I'm probably going to give her an unwelcome sermon, and we'll undoubtedly argue. If she keeps her apartment messy, I might recall the days her bedroom at home looked like Filene's Basement during its one-day sale. And I just might utter something smart-alecky. I can do all this because she's my daughter and although we can occasionally deliver wounding or seething remarks, there's no need to prove and re-prove our love for each other.

With any girlfriend of my son's, I would never be so honest; at the very least, I would meticulously choose my words. His girlfriend hasn't grown up in my home. I haven't pulled my hair out rushing her from school to practice or become agitated over her leaving the dishes in the sink or lectured her when she failed a test. In other words, a guy's mom and his girlfriend can start from square one.

Not only are they beginning fresh and new, but most boys' mothers tend not to pry too forcefully into the lives of the girlfriends. These same moms, however, pry with impunity into their own daughters' lives. They will go to any lengths to find out who a daughter sat with at lunch, or who else attended the party, or what is making her so grouchy. When it comes to their sons' significant other, they'll generally keep a respectful distance.

There's also a meaningful difference in the ways a daughter and a daughter-in-law react to a guy's mother. A daughter will probably ignore her mother if she tells her to push her hair back off her face or wipe off some of her makeup. But a son's significant other is hypersensitive to his mother's comments and is more likely to heed what the woman is saying. She may not agree, but she'll clearly hear her.

Another discrepancy exists in the frequency in which a mother expects to hear from her children. She may talk to her daughter every day. But she'll settle contentedly to hear from her daughter-in-law, or son's significant other, every few weeks or so.

Many of the moms and girlfriends I interviewed have developed a loving relationship with the "other" woman. For some of the girlfriends, a strained or lacking relationship with their own mother has led them to seek a close bond with their boyfriend's mom. And for many of the mothers, they find they are able to connect with the girlfriend even more than with their sons.

———

So while we talk about handling the difficult situations that arise out of the woman-to-woman dynamic between a guy's mom and his girlfriend or wife, we should also highlight the positives. Our love has no limits unless they are self-imposed. In fact, even as we age, the heart can continue to expand. It makes room for new offspring, new siblings, new friends, new puppies. It can surely find space for the new love of a loved one.

Keepsakes

1. His significant other wins first place or the game's over—for everyone.

2. A "whole" mom—one who has found happiness that's not reliant on her kids—finds it easy to love and to be loved.

3. If a guy's mom is single, everyone involved—the son, the girlfriend, and the mother herself—will find they have to work a little harder to overcome any guilt or sense of loss.

4. Sons and boyfriends should never avoid the melee, especially since they're at the center of it.

5. A mother wants someone who will make her son happy. A girlfriend just wants her to recognize that she does.

CHAPTER TWO

His Role: Burying His Head in the Sand Is *Not* an Option

A few summers ago I took my son and his then-girlfriend to a posh restaurant at the beach. They sat across from me, my son savoring his twenty-eight-dollar filet mignon (lucky for me he hates lobster) and his girlfriend discussing her intended career path after college. We talked about where she would go to graduate school—coincidentally, in the same city where she wanted my son to go to medical school—and where she would like to work; conveniently, in the same city where her father practiced; not to mention where she would like to live—close to her mother, far from me. In fact, the entire time we discussed these plans, which obviously affected my son as well as her, I glanced over at Noah. He seemed perfectly content devouring his steak, like a GI eating a home-cooked meal after a year of C-rations, rather than joining in the discussion.

I took my son's silence for both acceptance of his girlfriend's pronouncements as well as satisfaction for not being the one to have this emotionally charged conversation with his mother. I half expected him to finish his pricey repast, sit back, pat his belly, and belch. Thank God, I did something right in raising him.

This was June. If you had asked me then what Noah planned on doing with his life, I would have recounted that dinner conversation in which his immediate future was completely drawn out. So imagine my surprise a month later when he broke the news to me that the relationship was over.

"And why?" I asked.

"Because," my son replied, "she had my whole life planned out for me."

I reminded him about that evening and said, "I just assumed you agreed with her because you never said anything."

"No, Mom, you never asked me."

Okay, in my defense, as a mom I'm never quite sure how responsive my son will be to my questions, so I wait for one of his rare talkative moments when I interrupt everything to hear him emit. Once, I foolhardily stopped my bike in the middle of a heavily traveled road because I saw his name flash across my cell phone. I was not going to miss an opportunity for a son-initiated conversation. Most mothers know that a male child's willingness to converse gradually lessens with age (unless, of course, he needs our help) and can hit a virtual standstill just when we really need to know what's going on in his life.

> *Of all the animals, the boy is the most unmanageable.*
> —Plato

Confide in Me

Some young sons always confide in their moms, informing them of every crush, every slow-dance partner, and every text message. But somewhere along the way, certainly by the time they enter a serious relationship, most boys stop viewing their mother as their confidante. This change is necessary.

While you may miss the days your son used to confide in you, recognize that when he continues to do so after becoming involved in a serious relationship, that creates an unwholesome dynamic for everyone involved. Think back to your childhood. You refrained from confiding in your mother when a phrase like *Joseph should have told me his parents weren't going to be home* sparked an inquisition. That's how our sons feel. And can you blame them? If my son were to say in passing that his girlfriend preferred the Midwest to living near our home in the Northeast, he knows that would unleash a flurry of questions from me. "Does that mean she's moving back home? Does that mean you're moving away? Does that mean you two are breaking up?" So it's easier for him to leave much unsaid, to me at least, until he has something meaningful to report.

Nicci says her son would confide in her about his concerns regarding friendships and work until he met his current girlfriend. "He hardly calls me anymore now that he can talk to her," Nicci says. "That's great. But it doesn't mean I don't miss it a little bit."

The trade-off to Nicci giving up her role as confidante is that her son is happy. As she says, "He doesn't discuss worrisome issues with me now. I think that he's still close to me, but things have changed because he doesn't need me in the same way. He has her to confide in."

Linda, who says she talks to each of her married sons at least once a day, insists that the conversations are chatty and not embedded with private disclosures. "That's okay," she says, "because they shouldn't continue to confide in me."

If they did, their relationship with their wives would probably be suffering. A man who picks his mother to be his confidante is signaling a lack of trust in his significant other. Nothing will cause a romance to unravel more quickly than a loss of trust. As a mom, before you give your son an opportunity to unload his concerns, first suggest he consider why he

needs to. Make remarks that are not accusatory but will provoke thought. "Is there a reason you're discussing this with me
and not Lisa? If you're feeling the need to confide in me rather
than in your wife, maybe you two would benefit from speaking
with an uninvolved third party. I am much too close to you to
render an impartial opinion."

Meg knows that the fact that one of her four grown sons has
resumed confiding in her is a sign that things are not going
well in his marriage. He calls her to complain that his wife is
spending too much money on renovating their house. "He told
me she got thousand-dollar curtains for the kitchen. I think
he's just had it. He tells me these things because he knows I'm
safe. I'm not going to tell anyone or make him feel bad."

Like Meg, moms who find themselves as a son's sounding
board must refrain from making negative comments about his
wife. Such comments will be impossible to recant if the couple
resolve their problems and she remains in his—and therefore
his mom's—life. When Meg's son calls, she is very careful not to
appear judgmental, prefacing her remarks to him with, "Can
you believe curtains cost so much?" rather than the more
tempting, "What! Is she crazy spending money like that?"

"You validate your son's feelings," says Meg, "but you say
nothing that can't be retracted. You never say, 'You're right.
She's inconsiderate,' as much as you may want to."

As a girlfriend, it becomes uncomfortable to think your
boyfriend is confiding in his mother about your relationship.
Certainly, you want to rate so high in his life that he can't help
but tell his mom all about you, but there are distinct boundaries. While he can, and should, tell his mother about your job,
your expertise in the kitchen, your summer in Morocco, he
doesn't need to complain to her about your erratic sleep habits
or your uncontrollable urge to buy shoes. That's more than the
other woman needs to know.

If you suspect he's complaining to her about issues concerning your marriage or relationship, you need to confront him. Your relationship will never survive if either of you feels a need to go outside it to your moms. When it comes to their children, mothers cannot be objective, and if they are given a reason to distrust their child's significant other, they will find it impossible to change their feelings regardless of how their child changes his or hers.

That's part of Paul's problem. His candor about his wife's emotional issues has made it difficult for his mother to be impartial. "My mom is concerned with how I'm dealing with them. It's really tough being married to someone who is depressed and up all night crying. I'll talk to my mom about it. She knows it's one of the most difficult parts of my relationship. But I don't think my telling her about this colors her opinion of my wife. Definitely not. I think she's just being concerned about how I'm holding up." Actually, a mother will be affected by this information. She may love the girl, think she's sweet and kind, and knows she loves her son, but if she sees her son deteriorating in a difficult relationship, she's not going to be supportive. His talking to her about his wife's problems will not help the relationship between the two women.

As psychologist Lazaroff says, "It's important not to look for support where you've traditionally looked for support. Once you invite the mother or the mother-in-law into your business, you can't erase this. It's there permanently. Abusive tempers, sexual problems, emotional problems—if these exist, it is better for the man to seek outside help rather than confide in his mom." A mom, as she says, "doesn't have amnesia."

April purposely refrains from asking questions because she fears getting dragged into her son's rocky marriage. But Tom constantly seeks his mother's approval and continues to ask for her advice. When he complains about his wife, April says very little. "It's not my job to tell him what to do, but if he sounds upset and not happy, maybe I'll tell him he has to reevaluate."

It may be impossible for your son to fully appreciate the consequences of being in a poor relationship when he's entrenched in it. We all benefit from twenty-twenty hindsight. As my son says about his relationships: "There are things you see and I don't, and things I see and you don't. We both find different pros and cons." You should handle this the way April does, and not judge or criticize, or risk shutting off all communication with your son. Tell him something like: "I want nothing more than for this to work out for you both. If you haven't already, take some time to evaluate all your differences and make sure they won't matter later." Soon after I married my second, now ex-husband, I wondered if I had made a terrible mistake. We began facing insurmountable differences, including over how to raise our own kids and how to handle finances. A friend told me that so long as my husband and I held similar values, these other issues wouldn't matter. I realized we didn't, and in my case it was too late.

> *Boys are beyond the range of anyone's sure understanding,*
> *at least when they are between the ages*
> *of 18 months and 90 years.*
> —James Thurber

The Silent Treatment

You're a mom reading this and thinking, *Confide in me? I'd be happy if he just told me he was dating!* Remember, men generally do not gab as much as women, who often will talk to anybody about almost anything. (I'm actually privy to the knowledge that my girlfriend and her husband prefer to have sex in a hot tub rather than in bed and that another girlfriend snores so loud her husband now sleeps in the basement.) Men, on the other hand, would never reveal such intimate details, preferring instead to mention their sports injuries or car troubles. So what do you do if you have a son who refuses to talk, giving you no idea if he even has a girlfriend?

Lily sighs knowingly about this. She says her son "doesn't share" anything about his romantic life. When he was in high school, Lily became acquainted with male friends who frequently hung out at her house, but she had no idea he had begun dating. Even when he became serious with one particular girl, he not only didn't bring her home to meet his family, but didn't even mention her.

"He doesn't talk a lot," Lily says of her now twenty-five-year-old son. "I wasn't privy to this relationship, and she didn't come to our house. It was at least one or two months before I knew they were going out. He never came rushing home and said, 'Mom, I met this wonderful girl.' There's no announcement like there is in the female world."

There is not only rarely an announcement of a love interest from a son, but he'll have to consider her to be a "girlfriend" before he casually drops her name into a conversation. Sue was surprised to learn that her son had a girlfriend, a young woman who is now his wife. Her son introduced this woman to her as a professional colleague and a friend. It was only a short while later that he stunned his mom with the news that not only were they dating, but their relationship had become serious and they were about to become engaged.

Sons also seldom announce a breakup, waiting instead for Mom to notice something off kilter. I can always tell when my son's relationship with a girlfriend is over: He acts either a bit mopey or unusually enthusiastic. Whichever way, once I recognize a change in mood, I may say something like, "How's Abigail?" He'll always answer truthfully, apparently relieved that it's out in the open. What often follows is a vibrant conversation, the likes of which I haven't seen since before the relationship began. I move back into the position of number one female, at least until the next girl comes along.

Hope's son told her when he broke up with a girlfriend whom he had repeatedly criticized as being too "high-maintenance." But what he neglected to tell his mother, who disliked the woman, was that they resumed dating two years later. Since that time, she has become Hope's daughter-in-law.

So how does a mom encourage a normally uncommunicative son to open up about his social life? It's by first letting him know you're willing to listen and not to judge. You can start a conversation by asking: "Are you dating anyone right now?" If the answer is no, let it go. If the answer is yes, you can ask her name, how they met, and where she goes to school or what she does for a living. Leave the details or his expectations of the relationship up to him to divulge. As Linda, the mother of three sons, says: "My boys talk. The secret is that if you're quiet and don't pry, they'll talk."

If, no matter how delicately you handle the situation, your son won't divulge, then enlist the help of a third party. My friend always sends her son over to my house when she's trying to figure out his social life. He's too polite a guy to be rude to me. So I just come out and ask, "Are you seeing anyone now?" And then—as I'm sure he knows—I get on the phone to his mom.

The reason most boys consciously decide not to talk to their moms when they are considering whether to date a particular girl is that they don't want their decision to be clouded by their mother's judgment, and they certainly don't want her to talk them out of it. I've never known when my son had entered a relationship until it was already well under way. Recently we talked about his former girlfriends. "I had lots of them," he says. "I rarely told you about them. I didn't have to, because you figured them all out."

When he was in college, I had no idea whom he was dating unless he told me. Fortunately, if he thought a relationship had the potential to be serious, he didn't keep me out of the loop. (Thank you, Noah.) But when he was younger and had a girl-friend, if I couldn't tell by his actions, then I learned about it from the mothers of his female friends. Since daughters tend to talk a lot more than sons, it behooves all mothers of boys—particularly those sons in their teens—to befriend the mothers of their son's female classmates. You'll learn probably more than you want to know, as I did when one of his middle school girlfriends held an unchaperoned party (the parents were home when I dropped him off) and a few of the girls dared one another to skinny-dip in the backyard pool. Fortunately for my son, when I learned about this event from another girl's mom, he had already broken up with the hostess with the mostest.

Don't Ask, Don't Tell

Most of the young men I interviewed, although they love their mothers, try not to talk to them about their relationships for fear of being asked questions to which they themselves haven't yet found the answers. Joe, a twenty-eight-year-old graduate student, says he's reticent to discuss his girlfriend with his mom. Although he calls his mom once a week, he never talks about his relationship. "I'm reluctant," he says. "I don't want to call her nosy, but that would open the door to even more questions."

And opening the door to more questions is exactly what your sons want to avoid. It's not because they don't want you to know. They do. They just don't want you to needle them with questions that may make them rethink their feelings. They want to reach a conclusion on their own regarding a girl. Even Adam, who allowed his mom to influence his relationship with Allie, says he would not be affected by his mother's opinion if he really loved someone and she didn't. "I understand the impact or influence of having an opinionated mother," he says. "It can be a very difficult situation if you don't have your mother's support. I think it can suck in a lot of ways."

As much as I say I accept and respect my son's desire to keep his relationships to himself, if he isn't going to volunteer any information about a serious romance, I will always ask him a few need-to-know questions. "Are things going well with her? Does this relationship feel different from your last one?" I respond to his affirmative answers with casual approval. "That's good. She's a really great girl." And then I let it go. Not only do I not consider my questions too meddling, I feel that as his mother I'm entitled to know if he has feelings for someone, and once I do, I believe my son feels unburdened. I also settle for a yes or no response and don't force him to elaborate. More will come later.

Rebecca says when she asks her son the same sort of questions about his girlfriend, she gets: " 'I don't know. We'll see.' I don't think he admits to himself so he can't divulge to me." Fair enough. As mothers, you have to know how far to go with the questions you ask. Remember, refrain from asking for details because they will emerge eventually, either from your son or directly from his girlfriend. Your goal with a son who doesn't like to talk is to be respectful of his feelings toward this woman, and to let him know that you are aware he is involved in a relationship—and ready and willing to discuss it whenever he chooses. By giving him his necessary space, you help ensure that a time will come when he opens up to you, to tell you either they're in love or they're over.

Dr. Lazaroff agrees that a mother should be allowed to ask a few questions if her son isn't forthcoming. "I don't think there is anything wrong with a conversational question," she says. "I think it's up to the guy and the girlfriend to determine how much they want to share. Most people delicately stay away from money and sex questions because they are loaded and private. But you may ask: 'Do you want to keep living in the city? Do you think you might want to have kids someday?' Interrogation and bugging takes it to another level. To say, for example, 'You've been married six months, when are you going to have kids?'—that becomes intrusive." Mothers should always be considerate of what to ask and how to say it. You might ask them if they are thinking of buying a house, but you never say, "When are you going to stop wasting money on rent and buy a house or an apartment?"

One of Rebecca's sons has been living with his girlfriend for two years and has given no indication whether they plan to get married. So at some point Rebecca decided to ask. "He replied 'There's no need until we talk about having children.'" The next logical question was: *When is that?* Rebecca felt if he wanted to tell her more he would have given her a more revealing answer, so she let it go. "I don't nag for more than he wants to tell me. It's none of my business. I think it's her business and if she's happy living with him and not getting any other commitment, that's her issue. I am curious, though, how long she wants to wait with her biological clock."

She disliked her son's previous girlfriend for repeatedly breaking up with him and then insisting they get back together. "When he kept taking her back, I became concerned. That was frightening to me. So I said to him, 'Why are you doing this when she hurt you?' I had to open that avenue of conversation. He did what he did anyway and got hurt again."

According to counselor Ganz, engaging in this sort of discussion with your son is helpful and gives him an opportunity to get something off his chest. "Try to draw out his thoughts," she says—warning, however, to be careful not to say anything bad about the girlfriend. "Talk instead more about his own behavior."

If, rather than passing judgment, a mother can show her

support, she'll guarantee that her son will listen to her the next time around. Parents who've had one child go through a divorce are understandably more apt to voice their concerns if that child, or a sibling, enters a potentially destructive relationship. "I didn't speak up to my daughter who went through a terrible divorce, and now I speak up all the time," says Caroline. However, she is careful not to criticize her son's wife because "that's his Achilles' heel. He goes crazy." If she expresses any concerns, she immediately follows up with support for whatever decision he makes.

I wonder: If someone had told me their misgivings about my second husband before I married him, would I have listened? I do know one thing: After the divorce, I was all ears.

His Supporting Role

William was a junior in a big-city high school when he met Nina. She was cute, petite, and personable. He had never had a girlfriend before, and being the eldest of four—and the only son—he dreaded involving her with his inquisitive parents and younger sisters. So he didn't. Today, six years later and still in love with the same girl, William has finally begun including her with his family. He admits it would have been a lot easier had he started from the beginning.

"At first, it was embarrassing being the eldest child and having them meet her. Then it became laziness—it's gone on this long and it would be awkward to bring them together now. It's just easier to keep them apart than to deal with the consequences," he says.

A lot of sons think this way. They may date someone casually and the next thing they know they are in a serious relationship and Mom still hasn't met her. Now when he introduces her to the family, their relationship takes on a significance that promises a future. Everyone feels awkward because so much weight is brought to bear on this romance. The mother is wondering if this is *the* one, the sister is wondering what her brother sees in her, and the girlfriend is feeling scrutinized. Not the best environment in which to develop loving relationships among all the women in a guy's life.

William blames the uneasiness among his girlfriend, mother, and sisters on how he handled it initially. Although he would visit Nina at her parents' house, he purposely never invited her to his. "For the first several years I hid her away from my family for no real good reason. I didn't want to deal with all the family stuff—being the eldest kid and doing all the introductions—so I set up a tug-of-war between Nina and my family.

"I think that my mom has never had a problem with Nina," William adds. "It's just the fact that she was never around and I was always with her; that was a little difficult for everybody. In the end it was a bigger deal than it had to be."

Today he believes his girlfriend and his mother get along well—but this outcome has taken years and a gradual acceptance on his family's part that their relationship will likely turn into marriage. William says he has had a lot of conversations with both his mother and his girlfriend, conversations he found uncomfortable to have because he didn't know where they would lead.

A lot of men avoid taking this step, yet these sorts of discussions are necessary for bringing the women together. The man has to handle any complaints with diplomacy and never put the other woman on the defensive. He can't say, "Mom, you're rude to my girlfriend," without expecting to hear, "I'm rude? *She* barely says hello when she comes in the house!" And he can't say to his girlfriend, "My mother says you rarely acknowledge her when you see her," and not receive a similar response of "What! I offered to go out for lunch with her and she told me she was busy!"

The point is that no guy wants to aggravate the women he cares about, and he knows that if he has these conversations with either one, he will be lifting a floodgate and letting in a deluge that no amount of sandbags will stop. It's easy to understand why most guys prefer to remain ignorant and take any sort of polite conversation between the women as a gesture of mutual like and respect. The women know, however, that it is polite conversation and nothing more.

If the guy doesn't get involved, then this seemingly civilized communication among the females could just serve as a lid over a boiling pot of accusations, disapproval, and dislike that could blow at any time and leave some irreparable scars. William says, "I had a couple of very frank conversations with my mom explaining how Nina felt, and recognized some behavior by my mom that was not welcoming of her. She was cold and removed, and would give Nina mixed signals. But I think Nina didn't cooperate, either. She had it in her head that my family didn't like her and took everything that could be perceived in a certain way as evidence. So my mom would say something completely in friendship and Nina would say, 'I can't believe your mom said that to me, she doesn't like me.' That would cause me to turn a blind eye because I struggled with it."

It's taken William a while to realize that his confronting all the women in his life has actually helped create some harmony. "I had to convince Nina and my mother to get along. I've learned to manage it. From my mom, my sisters, and Nina, I take everything and give their fears and worries due time. But when I was younger, I overreacted, which did nothing but exacerbate the situation.

"If I could do it all over again, I would do it differently," he adds. "For one thing, I would act more enthusiastically to both sides about the relationship. That would have eased the tension. It is so gratifying to see your girlfriend get along with your mother—that makes life so much easier for everyone involved. They're thrilled. You're thrilled. You don't have to deal with the mess that would be otherwise."

As with William, most men worry over whether their mother and their girlfriend will get along, yet refuse to become involved in any conflict between the two females. That's nowhere-land for a guy. Imagine putting yourself in the middle of a football team's skirmish without protective equipment. It's much safer to watch from the sidelines. And because guys feel this way, they let it affect when and how they'll introduce all the women in their lives, and then how often they'll get them together. But not introducing a mother to a serious girlfriend is not an option— nor is continuing to keep them apart because they aren't fond of each other. Men need to understand that these conflicts will never go away unless something occurs to create favorable feelings toward the other woman. Remember that the bottom line for a mother, once she gets over her change in place in her son's life, is that her son is happy. If a girlfriend plainly makes a guy happy, eventually the mother will have to concede this. And if the mother is nice to the girlfriend, the girlfriend will be hard-pressed to dislike her.

Ganz agrees with the way William handled the situation by talking individually to each woman. She suggests that rather than bring everybody together, the man should speak to his mother and his girlfriend one-on-one to ascertain their concerns. The son/boyfriend obviously can't force everyone to like one another, but at the very least, she says, he can insist everyone be courteous.

"He should walk that fine line," Ganz says. "He should try to be positive with each one. Say, 'I know how you're feeling. But let's look at it this way.'" He should validate each woman's concerns and then try to explain why the other one acts the way she does. If you hurt your son's girlfriend's feelings by forgetting to invite her to a holiday dinner, your son should be able to say to you: "I know we've always had Thanksgiving with just us, but Sophie is a big part of my life now and it would mean a lot to me for her to join us." To Sophie, he could say, "I know how it hurts you that my mother forgot to include you. It hurts me, too, but I realize she didn't understand how serious we were and how important it was for me to have you there."

Joe says his biggest problem is not giving enough of his time to his mom and girlfriend. "It's a never-ending battle," he explains. "My experience with women is they are not very rational. No matter how much I explain it. They capitulate but I don't know if they are satisfied." It's not that women are never satisfied, it's that they want to feel loved and needed by what may be the most important male in their life. And a guy who can make them feel this way by being supportive will be rewarded with all the women in his life getting along.

Paul thinks he may be too frank with both his mother and his wife, and is beginning to believe he should be more circumspect. "I accidentally let it slip into a conversation that I was getting advice from my mom, and Jess's reaction was a little worried. 'Does your mom not like me? Why is she so concerned?'"

Men have to consider the complaints or comments they get from each woman before making a decision about what to convey to the other. If a girlfriend, for example, calls his mom a "bitch" or "obnoxious," a guy would never repeat that, nor would he tell his girlfriend that his mother thinks she's a "spoiled brat." These sorts of comments have as much staying power as a plastic bottle in a landfill and are just as tasteless. If, however, someone comments on a specific act or behavior that *could* be conceived as unintentional or inadvertent, that can, and should, be related. Perhaps the girl feels the mother is inconsiderate for failing to include her in an event—an easily rectifiable situation. Or the mother feels the girl is unfriendly because she ignores her whenever she comes over (maybe she's just shy). Rather than let these misperceptions continue, it is up to the man to resolve them.

Adam admits that he didn't give his mother and girlfriend an opportunity to develop any feelings—good or bad—toward each other because he kept them apart during his mother's visit. "I should have forced my mother to suck it up and be nice for a weekend, but instead I made the wrong decision. That was bad. That was beyond hurt. She didn't want to include Allie. At the end of the day, I don't have the support of my mom for Allie, and that's a problem." If Adam were to say to his mother: "Mom, I love you and want to spend time with you but it would mean a lot to me to include Allie in our plans. I really want you to get to know her," his mother would find it difficult to turn him down.

Robert knows what to say to his mother so that she recognizes the importance of his girlfriend in his life. There are no ifs, ands, or buts. "I'd say to my mom, 'This is my partner. This is the person I'm spending the rest of my life with. This is the person I love unconditionally and she loves me the same way.' My thought is my mom will not love her the way she loves me, but love her for loving me. And love her for committing her devotion and life to me. I think that's how it can work."

Robert also believes that if his mother is critical of his girlfriend and his girlfriend is bothered by it, they have to stop complaining to him and go to each other. "They can't have a meaningful loving relationship if they don't voice their opinion to each other. Every time they complain to me from now on, I will tell them to go to the other person. From my perspective, it's kind of logical. When you have a loving relationship, you talk about things that aren't always positive and you deal with the negative stuff. I'm not saying to duke it out. But if something hurts you, say 'When you say these things, it hurts. Is there something going on? Is there something I can do differently?'"

Dr. Lazaroff believes that Robert is on the right track; he is correct in saying the best way to work out a problem between two people is to have them work on it directly. However, she says, it should be orchestrated by the guy. He should cajole the two women into getting together to talk. If they meet for lunch, then he could join them for dessert. By helping them find a common ground, he isn't abdicating his responsibilities.

"Ideally, in a perfect world if people weren't defensive, it would be great to bring in the couple and their parents," Lazaroff explains. "But given that that is not realistic and given that this young man has to deal with all the people his whole life, it is better we strengthen him at the outset. This isn't going away."

Jenny says she has yet to have a one-on-one with her boyfriend's mother or sister and instead expresses her concerns through him. He always blames a difficulty between the women on himself, because he, like William, refuses to mesh his girlfriend with his family. I understand this. For the longest time, I didn't know my current boyfriend's family because he didn't want to combine these two parts of his life, which were operating just fine by themselves. When I insisted it was time I meet his mother and brother, both of whom I liked instantly, he was unnecessarily nervous.

Jenny says she used to be reluctant to tell her boyfriend that she felt uncomfortable around his mother and sister. Then two years into their relationship, she became so frustrated she told him how she was feeling. "I said I didn't feel acknowledged by his mom. I was a particularly special person in his life. If anything, I thought his mom was closer to his male friends than to me and I didn't feel I was extended any sort of special introduction into their lives." Her boyfriend understood and agreed to speak to his mother. After that, his parents started inviting Jenny to barbecues and family parties, and they began to accept that she constituted a major part of their son's life. Today the situation, though still somewhat awkward, has improved.

"When I spoke to him, he recognized it was an issue, and the fact that he decided to sit down and talk to his mother about it was a huge thing," Jenny says. "He told her I didn't feel welcomed in the family. And now I haven't brought it up lately. It just doesn't seem worth it. He thinks it's fine. It's okay but it could be better."

Unfortunately, even the guys who recognize the friction between their mothers and their significant others, and work to improve the situation, often get to a point of being battle-weary. If everyone is cordial, then they take that as mutual affection. They don't want to hear any more. At that point, like Robert suggests, it may be left to the women to handle themselves.

When I asked my son how a guy knows whether his mother and girlfriend are getting along, he said: "It's more a feeling; knowing that you and her and [his sister] Debra can go off and do something and I'm not worrying."

According to Lazaroff, the guy is often put in a position of hearing conflicting comments. "He will almost hear one voice about what the girlfriend is saying, that the other is too controlling, and then he might hear from the mother that the girl is a princess. And he has to weigh that feedback from both of them and really consider it and then decide how he feels and assertively take a position that is right or comfortable for him, not to please either one of them. That's the operative piece."

If he feels he is being influenced by both women, he has to remove himself emotionally and process the situation alone. For example, if his mother wants him to go into the father's business and the girlfriend wants him to go to dental school, he needs to ascertain what's best for him. If it's his father's business, then he will convey to his girlfriend that that is his choice. Lazaroff says, "He could tell her, 'I understand that you may feel that my mother is too controlling and my mom is dynamic and has strong feelings about what I should do in my life, but I do want what she proposes.' Even though the mother has that opinion, he is making up his own mind."

In the end, once a son enters a committed relationship, as William found, all the women in his life will benefit by being friendly to each other. Admittedly, from the male perspective, this is not easy to accomplish. "A girlfriend needs something different from a mother," notes my son, Noah, "and different from a sister. Frequently they can coincide, but sometimes they conflict. You have to make decisions that aren't going to please everybody. But when they all get along, it's nice. It definitely makes life easier."

I Married My Mom!

My friend Beverly describes her daughter-in-law as feisty, smart, spoiled, and assertive. Not surprisingly, that describes Beverly, too.

In fact, as I think about a lot of the mothers and daughters-in-law I know, I realize there is a striking similarity—not in appearance, necessarily, but in personality. A guy whose mom is strong and independent will probably have little patience for a girlfriend who is meek and clingy. Most men do not intentionally set out looking for their "mother," but since she is the female who raised them and she is the one they've grown to love and respect, it's only natural that they would seek a similar type of woman for their wife.

"I do think some people will marry one of their parents consciously or subconsciously," says Lazaroff.

Pam understands this concept. She says her own mother was critical and a bit of a nag, and she married a man who is also critical and harasses her to get things done. "So I married my mother and I'm cool with it. Now my son is marrying a bright girl. She even looks like I did when I was her age. There are things that are very similar, especially in terms of warmth and support and intelligence. He's with someone similar to me."

Ganz agrees that a lot of men marry their mothers. She says, "It's only a problem if the mother has a problem. Strong mom, strong girl. If he chooses someone with the negative personality of the mother—say, she's controlling—then it's going to be difficult." It may even be impossible. One of the women will have to take a step back and let the other one lead if there will be any hope for peace in that family. However, Ganz adds, "If he chooses someone who is pleasant and respectful, it's going to be wonderful."

Think of some of the former first ladies and their husband's mothers—Laura Bush and Barbara Bush; Rosalynn Carter and Lillian Carter; Hillary Rodham Clinton and Virginia Kelley. The sons who went on to become president of the United States were all extremely close to their moms—each one intelligent and highly capable. These men sought no less when they married.

So if you're having problems with the other woman, take a look in the mirror before you pass judgment. You may recognize the reflection.

————

The guy has the greatest responsibility in ensuring that the women in his life get along, yet he's the one most likely to shrink from it. He tries to ignore any simmering tensions between the two women rather than deal with them head-on. To that end, the son or the boyfriend is like an ostrich, the animal that myth says buries his head in the sand to escape detection. But just like the ostrich, he's pretty hard to miss.

Keepsakes

1. Moms should recognize that as their sons grow, they earn the right to more privacy, especially as it concerns their romantic relationships.

2. A son has a responsibility to keep his mom informed that he's seeing someone. Otherwise her imagination will run wild.

3. Men should be careful about confiding in their mothers about issues that affect their relationship with their significant other. While the man may move past such confessions, once a mother has been involved, she won't be able to.

4. If necessary, a man has to consider the concerns of both women and act as a mediator.

5. A mother-in-law may be difficult to love, but in some way, no matter how small, the man you love reflects off her.

CHAPTER THREE

Woman-to-Woman

Overjoyed that her twenty-five-year-old son finally had a girlfriend, Sally decided to welcome her to the family by cooking a meal to rival Giada De Laurentis. She searched four different markets for ingredients that were as difficult to find as they were to pronounce. She quizzed her son on his new girlfriend's interests in order to wrap a theme around the meal. As it turned out, his girlfriend loved animals. So in between picking up the Asian aubergines and the arborio rice, Sally bought a dog. The meal was a success. The relationship between her son and the girlfriend barely lasted four weeks. And the dog? Well, he's still not housebroken.

Certainly Sally meant well, but overeager and excessive actions like hers could be viewed by a girlfriend as a bit off-putting, intimidating, and even crossing the line. She's unintentionally given the younger woman a window into the future; a future potentially filled with a busybody—albeit well-intentioned—mother-in-law.

On the opposite side of the spectrum is the mother who

makes no effort to get acquainted with the girlfriend. As far as this mom is concerned, she continues her relationship with her son by dealing with him directly, asking him to stop over on his way home from work, or calling his cell phone so she doesn't have to speak to *her*. And she awaits the day he announces, "It's over." There is a happy medium here, one in which a mother can indulge both her son and his girlfriend or wife without infiltrating *Monster-in-Law* territory.

First thing to consider is the timing. The appropriate time for the two women to begin to develop a relationship should occur once the couple decides to date each other exclusively—a signal they may be getting serious. At this stage, the two women shouldn't go overboard with lavish attention and exorbitant presents; but perhaps make a phone call, send an email, or extend an invitation to lunch. If a birthday or holiday is about to occur, each should acknowledge it with a card, gift, or flowers. They should never leave it to the man to pass along their good wishes. It should come directly from the other woman.

Granted, creating any sort of relationship between the two women is impossible if both aren't willing to cooperate. If one of them reaches out only to be rebuffed by the other, everyone—from the son to the eventual grandchildren—will ultimately be affected. I tried to befriend the mother of a man I dated after I was widowed, but as hard as I tried I couldn't engage his dour (or was it sour?) mom. I don't want to say that she's the reason I finally broke up with him, but I wonder if in some ways she impacted that decision. Not only did she shrug off my friendly advances, but, in her presence, her son regressed to a young boy. He acted goofy and started telling jokes, like a stand-up comedian begging the audience for attention and a laugh. An only son, he was there for her entertainment, and I was that person who walks out at intermission, having had enough.

As the girlfriend, you may find that try as you might to connect with his mother, she remains resistant to your overtures.

She ignores you, making you feel invisible and insecure. With a mother like this, swallow your pride and make the first move. Initiate one-on-one time, inviting her to see a chick flick or calling periodically just to say hello. If she repeatedly snubs you, then at least you've tried, and her son will be aware of it. Since the woman's son is in love with you, she will ultimately come around to at least liking you. And if she doesn't, after you put forth such a great effort, that will be her loss.

In other instances, the mother is the one who reaches out only to receive little to no response. If the girlfriend is introverted and impossible to engage, then gradually try to pull her out. Maybe she feels threatened by your family for social, financial, or cultural reasons. (Don't underestimate this.) Or perhaps she feels like an outsider because you and your kids are so close. Make a point of getting together, just the two of you. In time she will open up. In fact, not only should you *always* ask your son how his girlfriend is doing, you should occasionally ask him to pass the phone to her. It may be a little awkward at first, but she will come to appreciate that you want to talk to her, too.

You are my sonshine.
—Author unknown

The Man as Proxy

Of course, our initial tendency when we meet the other woman is to funnel all our complaints through the guy, turning him into a kind of human strainer—only the material we need sifts through.

So he hears from his girlfriend: "Your mom didn't acknowledge my birthday."

And he hears from his mom: "Your girlfriend sits like a queen rather than help with the dishes."

And so he says to the girlfriend: "Mom's been so preoccupied with work, she even forgot my birthday!"

And to the mom: "Katie wants to help. She just doesn't want to get in the way."

Then he neatly wraps up the exchange by suggesting to his mom that they all go out to dinner to celebrate Katie's birthday, and informing his girlfriend that his mother would never ask for help but would be delighted if she offered.

If it's the first time these issues are brought up, it's easier to mention them to the male rather than directly confront the other woman. Maybe she didn't realize and a gentle reminder from the guy will rectify the situation. But in time, if the relationship between the son and his significant other is to continue, the two women will have to face each other and stop using the man as their conduit. Besides, the danger in repeatedly using the male as the intermediary is that he can be manipulated easily by a remark from either woman. Most men are vulnerable to subtle digs coming from someone they love.

Joe's mother takes advantage of opportunities to speak to her son alone just so she can disparage his girlfriend, Halley. And she knows exactly how to provoke. Aware, as we all are, how important looks are to a guy, upon meeting the younger woman for the first time, Joe's mother nonchalantly remarked: "Your girlfriend is very plain looking."

There are *no* circumstances in which a mom should criticize the looks of her son's girlfriend. Remember, he chose her. Even when she comes covered in tattoos and body piercings, choose nonjudgmental phrases like: *She must be artistic.* Or *she must have a high tolerance for pain.* But never call her "plain." To a male, that translates to "ugly," and there's no lower blow.

This comment from Joe's mother, which masks a deeper resentment toward his beautiful girlfriend, caused Joe to stop talking to his mom. His mother retaliated immediately. Under the pretext of discussing corsage colors for the prom, she phoned Halley's mother. After an obligatory, polite greeting, Joe's mother declared: "Make sure your daughter doesn't get too attached because my son just takes girls to the school dances and dumps them."

"That's what Halley told me," Joe says. "I asked my mother if she said that, and she didn't deny it. I told her to stop making ridiculous comments like that, but that didn't stop her."

Joe never actually witnesses his mother's snide comments to Halley because she usually unloads them when he's not around. And Halley, at least so far, has been too respectful of his mother to reply in kind. By her actions, his mother has accomplished very little other than to appear petty and jealous and to sadly distance herself from her son.

I realize there are some moms and some girlfriends or wives who will not only refuse to befriend the other woman but also try to turn the man against her. This is not only selfish, it's pitiful. You both love him and, hopefully, have his best interests at heart. If you see a problem with the other woman, look at yourself first. Is there anything you could do to improve this relationship?

Kelly can relate to Halley's situation. Her boyfriend's mom enjoys remarking on her son's previous girlfriends, inferring that Kelly will soon be joining their ranks. "She wouldn't dare say anything in front of her son," Kelly says. "Instead she says it when we are alone, like when I'm at his house and he goes upstairs to change. I'll be sitting at the kitchen table minding my own business and she'll give me a dig. I was only sixteen when we started dating, and I'm quiet, so I don't say much in response."

On the few occasions her boyfriend is present when his mother makes comments to Kelly, he either tunes them out or doesn't realize their intent. "One time when he had just come home from school, I walked in the house with him. His mom said, 'Oh, Ben, you're home.' And then she saw me. 'Oh, and there's your sidekick.' I was pissed off. Ben said, 'She's just joking.' He defends her a little bit. Sometimes when she makes mean comments to me, and I tell him about it, he says she's just lonely."

She's so lonely that in order to spend more time with her son, she persistently insists she join them for dinner—her treat. Sometimes they accept, but on one occasion, when Kelly and Ben had planned a quiet, romantic dinner alone, her son actually told his mom she wasn't invited to come along. That was a tiny breakthrough in Kelly's mind.

"Sometimes his mother will say to him, 'Oh, honey, I made your favorite just for you.' She'll make him certain things like beef stroganoff. She buys him stuff at the store so she can send him home with a care package. That bothers me a little bit—because I can't compete with that. It's also gross, like she's in love with him."

Although she's not "in love" with him, she does adore him. That's being maternal, and it's perfectly normal. And although I'm not defending the rest of Ben's mother's actions, what mother doesn't make a child's favorite meal or pack him a care package if he's going back to school or to his apartment?

Kelly admits that her own mom adores her little brother—"but he's only twelve!" she says as way of justification. I assure her, her mother's feelings won't change when he's twenty-one, or forty-one.

> *You never meet your mother-in-law on the day*
> *that you are well dressed.*
> —Creole proverb

The Face-Off

Before you can bypass the male and go directly to the other woman, which is your ultimate goal, you have to understand your boundaries. Developing a relationship through friendly correspondence including email, or chatting over lunch, is one thing—and a good thing—but confronting each other because you're not satisfied with the predictable inaction on the part of the guy is an invitation for trouble.

You need to have established a trusting connection with the other woman before earning the right to question or criticize her directly. And that can take months or even years. Remember, a woman can challenge her own mother and a mother can challenge her own daughter without devastating their mutual love. However, even in the best of circumstances, the relationship between a woman and her son's significant other has the ability to unravel over a single hurtful comment. So, while you should not depend on the male as a conduit, until you have a good relationship with the other woman, think twice before confronting her directly.

Sometimes a girlfriend finds she can't use her boyfriend as the go-between because the issues she needs to discuss are about him. While it's tempting to consult his mother—"Has he always been such a slob?"—don't take your relationship problems to her. If you and he have issues, see a therapist or work them out yourselves. The women (and that includes sisters) who were in his life before you arrived will commit to memory anything you say, even if it's in a fleeting moment of anger. Betty, who has two sons of her own, used to confide in her husband's mother and sisters about her unstable marriage. "I made the mistake as a young bride when I felt so disheartened and couldn't get him to change that I would look for support from his mother and sisters. I shared issues with them in the hope they might tell him off. In the end, he resented that his mother and sisters butt into his business and he was pissed at me for bringing them into our lives."

Dr. Lazaroff says, "I think the girlfriend has to be careful about going to the mother about certain things. It's okay if it's general information like telling them where you had dinner or your plans for the weekend. But never discuss your relationship problems." You'll almost always be the one at fault.

There are also the mothers-in-law who communicate with their sons, purposely sidestepping the wife and avoiding a face-off. But eventually this will feel devious and manipulative, and when the two women ultimately speak their conversation will be bloated with spiteful accusations and bad feelings. Marie's relationship with her mother-in-law has deteriorated to this point. She says her husband's mom calls her son at work or on his cell phone to avoid talking to her. For a very long time, Marie tolerated this underhandedness, until her life became stressful and her patience spent. "We had a new baby and both of us lost our jobs. We were paralyzed. We had a mortgage. We had had a plan. Now we had nothing. Then his mother called my husband and said, 'You have to pay more attention to me.' That was our first confrontation. I called her directly and said, 'We have to set ground rules. I don't like how you talk to my husband. You may have been the number one woman in his life before, but now you're a distant third.' She screamed: 'Are you calling me a bad parent?' I said, 'You're not a model I want to follow.'"

Furious with Marie, the mother-in-law immediately called her son to complain. "He's incredibly laid-back and reflective," Marie says of her husband. "He's committed to doing the right thing. But he doesn't know how to get away from her. He doesn't defend her. He sticks up for me." The relationship between Marie and her mother-in-law has worsened.

Marie says, "I told her, 'You back off or you'll never see your granddaughter and you won't see your son. He may be yours biologically, but he picked me.' She said to me, Who the hell was I to be calling her? And I told her, 'Don't you dare tell my husband. He doesn't know I'm making this call. You've twisted him to a place where he is physically sick. If you love him, you'll leave him alone.'"

Once a relationship between the two women hits a low point like this, it seems as though it can never recover. But it can. It may take months or even years for the women to reconnect over a life-changing family event like a death, a marriage, or a grandchild's birth, or when each woman feels more secure within her own life. Amy has experienced this. She stopped speaking to her mother-in-law following an argument in which Amy was blamed for her and her husband's marital problems. Ten years later, when Amy's eldest child got married and her in-laws came to the wedding—in the drunken light of the happy occasion—they began talking again. Older and wiser, not to mention a mother-in-law herself, Amy has resurrected her relationship with her in-laws. "It's great now," she says.

But Marie is years away from this point. All civilized boundaries between her and her mother-in-law have been obliterated—the boxing gloves are off. It may take a significant incident in either woman's life—like the mother-in-law getting remarried—or in the son's, for them to repair the damage.

Kelly says that, like Marie, her boyfriend's mom had repeatedly ignored her, addressing only her son when they were together. "Once I called her to invite her to dinner, just the two of us," Kelly says. "But she said, 'Why? Why do you want to go out?' I tried to be nice. I said, 'I haven't seen you in a while.' She was so rude about it." Despite the slight, Kelly persevered until her efforts gradually began to pay off. His mom now initiates conversations with her when she's over at her house, even if it's to pump her for information. "It can be annoying. It's nonstop questions. When she does the same thing to Ben, he tells her to stop. But I find myself telling Ben to leave his mom alone. I tell him to stop because 'She's your mom.' Who knows, I actually think she might be starting to like me." She probably is. By defending her, Kelly is becoming her ally.

Although in the case of Marie and Kelly, the guy's mother has handled communications poorly, sometimes it's the younger woman who does. As a gesture of friendship, Cindy took her pregnant daughter-in-law and her daughter-in-law's friend, who had recently had a baby, out to lunch. During the predictable discussion about childbirth, the friend revealed that her husband's mom had joined them in the delivery room. Cindy's daughter-in-law roared, "What the hell were you thinking to let your mother-in-law in the delivery room?" And then she turned to her mother-in-law and said, "Don't get any ideas."

"She could have phrased it differently," Cindy says. "I said I never expected to be in the delivery room. I don't know how I would have felt if she had asked me if I wanted to come in. If she had offered, even if I had turned her down, I would have liked it. She speaks her mind to anybody. The things she says that I take as an insult, she thinks she's just being honest. She says we can say anything to each other because we're so close. Not true. She can say anything to me. I sure as hell don't think I can say anything to her."

But what if Cindy tried? She could have said to her daughter-in-law, "It's your pregnancy and delivery and I completely respect your wishes. But when you speak that way to me, it's hurtful and disrespectful. You could simply have said, 'Mom, I hope you don't mind if you're not in the delivery room. I'm most comfortable keeping it private.'"

A comment like this is not accusatory or threatening—it's a statement that says you are entitled to respect, which you are. And whether you are the mother of the guy or his significant other, no one has any right to treat you otherwise.

Like Cindy, a lot of moms are reluctant to speak so honestly to their sons' wives or girlfriends for fear they will be shut out of the son's life completely. And a lot of the girlfriends are disinclined to talk back to the mothers out of a learned respect for their elders and because they know it may anger their sons. But speaking honestly—so long as it is reverential and considerate—will eventually result in a decent relationship between the two women.

Amy has learned from her once tense relationship with her in-laws how to be a good mother-in-law and to communicate directly with her daughter-in-law. Last Christmas holiday, she invited her son and his new fiancée to Christmas Eve dinner. When Amy learned of the younger woman's plans to leave early to go to a bar, she confronted her. " 'You're going to go to a bar on Christmas Eve?' I asked her. She said, 'Well, maybe.' I said, 'That would really bother me. If you're coming for dinner, I would like you to stay to celebrate Christmas.' " A few days later when the couple arrived for dinner, the fiancée ignored Amy. "It was clear she was avoiding me."

But Amy decided not to let this fester. As soon as the holiday was over, she called her future daughter-in-law. "I told her, 'You walked into my house and you didn't acknowledge me. This is my home. That is unacceptable. Whether you want to say 'Merry Christmas' or 'Go to hell,' you have to acknowledge my existence. If we're going to have a good in-law relationship we can't do things to hurt each other. I didn't talk to my mother-in-law for ten years and I don't want to put my son in the middle.' We cleared the air and came to an acceptance of each other's presence in my son's life." It's been a year since the wedding, and the two women have been getting along great.

Amy laid the groundwork for a mutually respectful relationship with her daughter-in-law. It doesn't matter which woman initiates this, but the earlier one does, the sooner the two of them can create a solid friendship. Standing on ceremony, like Cindy and Kelly do, may help prevent fireworks but it doesn't prevent bad feelings that fester and deepen until it's nearly impossible for the two women to connect.

Although Caroline doesn't like the way her daughter-in-law

parents or tidies her home, she works so hard at communicating with her that the two of them get along well. In fact, her daughter-in-law usually confides more in Caroline than she does in her own mother.

Another reason for a mother to develop a rapport with her son's girlfriend or wife is that men often don't like to talk. So, if you rely solely on your relationship with your son to find out what's going on in his life, you may be left in the dark. When I first found myself alone with one of my son's girlfriends I was reluctant to ask questions about their plans, or their friendships, or how things were going at school or work. But when I finally did, I learned a lot about my son. And I mean details. I learned that one of his friends was having problems at home and my son was helping him. I learned that he wanted to go to graduate school in environmental science. I learned that as a way to save energy, he doesn't always flush the toilet. (This I would have been happier not to know.) The point is, I learn more from his girlfriends than I ever do from him. When you ask a young woman how school is going, you'll hear about her irritating roommate, or her favorite class, or how one of her friends got pregnant and dropped out. If you ask your son how school is going, he'll say "Good" with as much monotone and lack of emotion as is semantically possible.

So in order for me to stay connected to my son, I have to have a relationship with his girlfriends. We don't have to be bosom buddies or quasi mother–daughter, but we do have to communicate, respectfully.

Each Biting Her Tongue

Meg has four sons and four daughters, all married with children. That translates into four daughters-in-law and numerous sisters-in-law, the permutations of which increase exponentially like breeding mosquitoes. And some might say, with as much sting and bite. As frustrated as she can become with her sons' wives, she never criticizes them—at least not to their faces—or confronts them. Even when one son complains about his wife's expensive house renovations, Meg knows what she has to do: bite her tongue. "I never confront her. She's a tremendous spendthrift, especially with this renovation of their house. She doesn't even want me to see it."

Meg disapproves of another daughter-in-law's practice of sitting and reading a magazine when she comes to visit rather than help her with the dishes. Instead of stewing about this, Meg should ask her to help. "Would you mind drying?" she could say, giving the younger woman an opportunity to get up and lend a hand. Maybe her daughter-in-law feels awkward in her mother-in-law's house, and thinks she can be most helpful by staying out of everyone's way. Once asked, if she refuses to get up from the sofa, then that's an entirely different situation.

If you're the significant other, you should offer each time you visit your boyfriend's mom, and don't assume that because she refused your help the last time, this will always be the case. Repeat your offer to clear the table or wash the dishes—whatever is needed so everyone is reminded that if you're not helping, it's because of their insistence and not out of your inconsideration.

Another of Meg's sons is married to a sweet woman who has a pharmacy degree yet has never worked. The couple has struggled financially. "My son commutes over an hour because his wife won't move. I stay quiet other than to say to my son that 'the commute must kill you.' I avoid confrontation with her at all costs." Meg also rarely sees the wife of her youngest son who visits his mom once a week by himself. "Even though it means she and I don't talk, I do appreciate her for letting him do that," Meg says. "It would have burned me up if my husband had visited his mom that often."

Incidentally, this is another of those gestures that should be recognized and appreciated by the mother. Once your son marries, and especially after he starts a family, he should not be expected to return home on a frequent basis. If he does, you have his wife to thank.

To ensure a good relationship with the wife, mothers of sons do need to know how to pick their battles. If you stay out of decorating issues and dog-rearing habits, you might be trusted to babysit your grandchildren, which is much more important. Take this easy test: If it's not harmful to your son, let it go. The beauty of hot pink paint in the dining room is in the eye of the beholder. Accept the fact that getting your daughter-in-law to like earth tones is a waste of time. Sue finds that she and her daughter-in-law, whom she describes as very independent, have different tastes, so she was a little reluctant to go with her to buy baby clothes. "I thought, *How ugly can baby clothes be?*" Sue says. "Well, apparently my daughter-in-law has figured that out." Sue wisely kept her mouth shut and enjoyed the time spent with her daughter-in-law. Later, when her son and daughter-in-law bought a new dining room set, they asked Sue what she thought of it. It was massive and hideous. "I didn't like it at all. But all I said was: 'That table is really large. It's going to serve a lot of people. Christmas dinner at this table is going to be wonderful.'"

Comments like this have guaranteed Sue a place at that dreadful table every holiday—with her son at one end and her grandchildren at the other.

Neat, meticulous Cindy always keeps her feelings to herself. When her son and daughter-in-law moved into their first house, her son returned to work and left the job of unpacking the boxes to his wife. But weeks went by and none of the boxes was opened and emptied. "It affected my son and I wanted to kill her," Cindy says. "It's chaos there. Boxes still remain unpacked. They lived like this week after week and my son told me he didn't like going home. It's like a storage facility." So Cindy called her daughter-in-law and offered to come over to help unpack. Initially the daughter-in-law agreed, but as the day got closer she changed her mind. "Then I thought, *You're on your own*. It was a hard lesson for me to learn."

There's another lesson here. Mothers too often let their sons get away with not taking their share of the responsibility. You get so used to making their beds or fixing their lunch so they don't miss the school bus, you forget they are more than capable of doing it themselves. For some, this transfers directly into adulthood as you continue to do their laundry or buy them groceries. You can end up creating a man who expects his wife to take over his mother's role. And while that is their issue to work out themselves, you certainly can't place the blame on your daughter-in-law.

To Cindy's credit, she learned to stay out of the unpacking issue (three years later, most, but not all, of the boxes have been emptied) and has salvaged a relationship with her daughter-in-law.

The Gift Horse and Her Mouth

Last Christmas, Kelly bought Ben's mom a pair of silver earrings that cost a hundred dollars, a dear amount on her salary. When everyone sat down to open their presents, Ben's mother unwrapped Kelly's gift, peeked inside the box, and said nothing. The next day Kelly told Ben that if his mother didn't like the gift, she would return it and give her a hundred dollars to spend on something else.

No matter what Ben's mother thought about the earrings, she should have thanked Kelly immediately. Even if she didn't like them, or if she felt embarrassed because they were more costly then the gift she had bought Kelly, she still should have shown her appreciation.

Several months later, Ben's mother gave Kelly a blouse. Kelly thanked her profusely for the present—but when she hung it in her closet, she noticed it was moth-eaten. Revolted, she threw it out. She decided not to tell his mom, who to this day thinks she loved the gift.

Both women have an obligation to show gratitude for any gift the other one gives them, unless it is really in poor taste or just completely thoughtless (we're going to assume the moth holes were uninvited). I was with a friend when her mother-in-law handed her a fortieth-birthday present. It was a size extra-large sweater emblazoned with a tennis racket and the words, TENNIS IS MY RACKET. My friend is neither an extra-large nor a fan of or participant in the sport of tennis. Nor was she surprised that her self-centered mother-in-law was so far off the mark. Still she thanked her, and exchanged the sweater for a belt.

Meg had given an expensive set of sterling silver—a family heirloom—to her son to give to his wife. "A month went by and I hadn't heard anything, so I said to my son, 'Did she like the silver?' He said, 'Oh yes, she's thrilled.' A week later I got a thank-you note from him and at the bottom she wrote, 'Thanks a million. We'll always remember you for it.' That took its toll on me. I was upset. I expected a phone call the next morning. I don't know if she even knows the worth of the silver."

I can't impress this enough: Something you consider a small gesture—even if you would have preferred silverware from Tiffany's—when it comes from the other woman, must be acknowledged immediately, and with great fanfare. And although I would never discourage anyone from actually writing a thank-you note, nothing beats a phone call. It forces the two women to connect one-on-one.

Gift giving is inherent with problems. I've always put a lot of thought into the gifts I've given my son's girlfriends. But I can sometimes tell when they open them that they are feigning delight. Truth is, I probably do it myself. Still, acting as though you like the gift, whether you're the mother or the son's significant other, is necessary regardless of what you really think of it.

Not all relationships require gift giving. A decision to give a present to the other woman should be based on the commitment level of the couple. If you, as the girlfriend, have been dating someone for a while—which is a period long enough that you call him your boyfriend—then his mother should acknowledge your birthday with a present, and you should acknowledge hers with one.

This also raises the issue of whether a gift should come from just you or be included in your boyfriend's present to his mom. Once the two of you have entered into a serious relationship—and especially if you're married—the gift should come from you both. If he leaves your name off the card, then he is helping to create a schism between you and his mother. Even if your name on the card is purely symbolic, its omission not only speaks louder but also gives the other woman permission to consider you a nonentity.

Jenny would just be happy to receive a gift from her boyfriend's mom. Despite the length of time Jenny has been seriously involved with her boyfriend—seven years—and the frequency with which she now sees his family, she says the mother makes her feel even more insignificant by never acknowledging her birthday with a present. "I just try to explain it away," she says. Jenny believes when they are married his mom will finally recognize her birthday just as she does her son's and her daughters'. If she doesn't, even her son will notice the discrepancy, especially if Jenny makes certain that she is included on every gift or card he gives his mom—and not just on her birthday, but on Mother's Day as well.

————

Although the couple's relationship is paramount, the relationship between the man's mother and his significant other ultimately affects the happiness of everyone involved. Knowing when to reach out, when to keep thoughts to yourself, and how to be supportive can guarantee successful relationships all the way around. Each woman has her own role to play, and sometimes that may require giving an Oscar-winning performance.

Keepsakes

1. Just because the other woman isn't receptive to you doesn't mean you don't try. You just try a little harder.

2. Be selective on the occasions you use the guy as the go-between. It's too easy to avoid the other woman when you do.

3. The two women must know their boundaries. Even if they become close, marital problems are never to be discussed with his mom.

4. Mothers should carefully pick their battles. Never interfere over decorating or dog rearing. In the end, they matter very little.

5. Love, love, love that birthday present.

CHAPTER FOUR

Guess Who's Coming
to Dinner?

You're a compulsive, organized housekeeper. She's an incorrigible slob who believes it's environmentally sound to wash dirty dishes only after they start sprouting their own food. You match your shoes to your bag and wouldn't be caught dead wearing white after Labor Day. She thinks flip-flops work for every occasion and proudly admits to owning only one dress, *an unbelievable find!* from a flea market. You're a vegetarian. She grew up hunting game. You never miss a Pilates class, she personifies "couch potato." Or—horrors! You're a Republican. She's a Democrat!

And I haven't even touched on the *really* divisive issues: culture, religion, and her prior marriage. The possibility a son will introduce his mother to someone she isn't expecting—especially since she's expecting a kinder, gentler version of herself—is greater today than ever before. Numerous opportunities exist for him to meet, and fall in love with, a woman who is much older or much younger, who's been married before, or who's been raised in a different culture or religion.

As the potential bride, you know that your differences with your boyfriend have not corrupted your relationship. He loves your three-year-old son from your first marriage. He's perfectly content forgoing a Hanukkah menorah for a Christmas tree, and if your idea on Thanksgiving is to trim a custom-shaped tofu bird, he will happily adjust. After all, he fell in love with who you are. So why can't his mother see that?

As a mother, but more significantly as a wife yourself, you believe that a successful marriage requires concentrated effort and patience and that significant differences in background can make a union even more challenging. Disagreements between a couple can certainly fray their marriage, but those can be over any issues—financial, sexual—and not necessarily over religious or cultural diversities. In fact, a couple coming from dissimilar backgrounds face their differences well before they decide to be married in a church or a temple. Their marriage will be based on an appreciation and respect for each other's customs. Ignited with such values it is less likely to go down in flames.

However, if as a mom you see red flags as early as with the wedding planning, you may feel inclined to express your concerns. Can you? Yes, at least initially, and so long as you can discuss them without bias or emotion. As impossible as this sounds, it is the only way that you will be heard and, even more important, that you will hear your son. Make your concerns about the couple, not about you. It doesn't matter that you're uncomfortable introducing your purple-tressed, vegan daughter-in-law to your bridge group. What matters is whether her uniqueness will effectively jeopardize, or enhance, her marriage to your son. Their future decisions—from which religion to embrace, if any, to whether to have children—will not involve you, so this is your time to put in your nonjudgmental two cents with a firm "I support you no matter what" at the end. If things work out for your son and this woman, you *will* be delighted, and if they don't, you haven't backed anyone into a corner, especially yourself.

When I broke the news to my Jewish parents that I was marrying a Gentile, my mom broke down and cried, and my dad turned to my soon-to-be-husband and said, "A father dreams about his daughter getting married." And without saying another word, it was fairly clear, my husband didn't figure in that dream. But he did in mine.

Despite this initial reticence, my parents ultimately permitted themselves to get to know him and love him until our difference in religion was no longer an issue. The result: They kept their daughter, their son-in-law, and their grandchildren very much in their lives.

> *Every mother hopes that her daughter will marry a better*
> *man than she did, and is convinced that her son will never*
> *find a wife as good as his father did.*
> —Martin Anderson-Nexo, author

Wouldn't Be *My* Choice

When I asked moms what they thought of their sons' girlfriends, many of them replied noncommittally, "Well, she wouldn't be my choice." The truth is, most mothers spend little time envisioning whom their sons will eventually marry until they're introduced to a likely prospect. It's at this point that they, even subconsciously, expect her to reach an unattainable standard of perfection, which consequently exposes her weaknesses. If they could design her from the ground up—or the heart out—like a robot, they would pick the following for their sons:

- Someone smart, but not so smart as to show him up;
- Someone pretty, but not so attractive that other men look at her;

• Someone capable—she can run a house, work a job, raise a family—but not so capable she doesn't revere your son. Or eclipse his mother.

Lily admits she wondered about her son's choice in a girl-friend. "To begin with, it was such a novel idea that he had a girlfriend. I didn't evaluate her. I found her personable, bright, very polite, and well mannered." Still, with all these attributes, Lily says, her background was so different, "I found it interest-ing that he chose her."

Cindy echoes Lily's feelings about her own son's selection. "It would not be who I would have picked," she says. "I watched him pick someone who wouldn't nurture him. I like her. I just didn't like her dating my son." This raises another point. As with Cindy and Lily, moms may actually like the woman their son brings home, they'd just prefer she was someone else's girl-friend. I get along great with the girlfriend of my son's friend, Brian. But I'm neither her mother nor her future mother-in-law. With her, my expectations and standards are completely relaxed, if not indulgent. She admits to drinking too much freshman year of college. I respond co-conspiratorially with my own first-time-away-from-home experience. She tells me she had a crush on her biology teacher. I reminisce about the guy with the cute butt who taught me in landscape design school. (Really, you couldn't help but notice as he led our class through the woods.) I don't judge her at all. So in her eyes, I'm way cooler than Brian's mom. I don't let the flattery blind me to the fact that my own son's girlfriend probably thinks Brian's mom is way cooler than me.

So long as we—both the man's significant other and his mom—believe a woman has no intimate bearing on us, we find it easier to like her. Even in situations where we may have known and liked the female at one time, our feelings about her will change once she becomes a potential mother-in-law or daughter-in-law. In Cindy's case, years before her son and his girlfriend began dating, they had been neighbors. Cindy had always considered the little girl next door very personable, especially when she doggedly insisted Cindy buy a month's worth of Thin Mints so she could earn another Girl Scout badge. She was cute and feisty as a child, but when fifteen years later she became a member of the family, those darling attributes translated into ego and stubbornness. Same person. Different role.

April, too, thinks her son's new wife is charming, but her unstable emotional state worries her. The young couple met at work and fell in love almost instantly. "When I first met her we said hello and she looked at me and said, 'I'm in love with your son.' They had just gotten together two weeks before. What do you do with that statement? It just went much too quickly. I can see why he's attracted to her. When we're together, I like being with her. When we're not, I think, 'Why did she come into my son's life?' and I feel guilty for thinking that."

Although as a mother you tend to be very critical of your son's choice, you do need to try harder to understand what attracts him to her. Psychologist Beatrice Lazaroff says, "Maybe the mother and sisters don't feel this girl is right or they are disappointed in his choice. It's a lot harder to get excited about someone they aren't thrilled about. But you accommodate. Speaking as a mother, I think there is an ideal person you would imagine for your child, but the reality is that may not be with whom they end up falling in love. Analyze the good in the person, even if she is not who you would pick. You have to respect your son's choice."

I agree. You've imparted on this young man all the values and morals that are important to you. Armed with that richness, he is bound to choose someone wonderful, at least where it matters most: in his eyes.

Amy admits that she liked a lot of her son's other female friends much more than the one he began dating in high school. "She wasn't the one I pictured my son with," says Amy. When the girl cheated on her son while away at college, Amy, suppressing her anger, gave her son carefully worded advice. "He called from school and he sounded like he was crying. I was relieved it was about a girl and not about school. I said all the right things: 'If it's meant to be . . . I know it hurts . . . You have a new chapter in your life.'"

But to herself, she rebuked the girl as despicable and felt relief that the relationship was over. Then, two years later, her son called to announce that they had resumed dating and were in love. "I was blown away. How all of a sudden do his feelings go from one place to another? I questioned it. But I didn't say that to him. I just told him to be careful. Just be a little guarded. I tried not to take away the happiness he was feeling."

Amy's decision to accept her son's choice has resulted in her maintaining a close relationship with her son, and with that girlfriend, who has since become her daughter-in-law.

When your son asks for your opinion of his new girlfriend, you should reply honestly but with judicious attention to your words. In the event this relationship becomes permanent, you won't be able to retrieve any negative comments. And since your son has asked, he will listen to—and remember—everything you have to say. If he doesn't seek your opinion, and you tell him anyway, he'll be disgruntled and will more than likely stop sharing any information with you.

When Hope's son asked what she thought of the woman he brought home, Hope considered the consequences of her response and then said: "'You can see she's a daddy's girl. She knows what she wants. She's bright. She's demanding. Somewhat spoiled. Maybe even a bit high-maintenance.' He said, 'You hit the nail on the head.' I think if I hated her, I wouldn't have told him. It was still the beginning of the relationship and they had to see if it would work out."

Fortunately, a lot of moms are introduced to girls whom they adore, and the feeling is mutual. Both Linda and Nicci liked their sons' girlfriends from the very beginning. "We clicked," says Nicci. "She was very warm and friendly and down to earth. It was amazing to see him so happy to like somebody. She really adores him and I had been worried that he wouldn't find someone who would cherish him." And Linda adds, "We liked her immediately and thought she was good for our son."

Even when you're not convinced this young woman suits your son, you have to give their relationship a chance to percolate. They might discover they aren't meant for each other, or they might find a way to forge a strong union despite their differences. Your thoughts are important to your son, but he doesn't need to know she's not who you would have selected.

Besides, can a son's girlfriend ever be good enough in his mother's eyes? Depending upon which woman is asked, the response will differ. The boy's mother, bent on appearing gracious and high-minded, might say, "Of course." The girlfriend, aware she is snatching the mother's precious son, might say without hesitation, "No way." There are exceptions to this, of course, such as in cases in which a son has rarely dated and the mother is thrilled that he finally has a girlfriend, or in which the son has struggled with issues, perhaps professionally or emotionally, and the mother sees the girlfriend as a godsend. Or, in situations in which, as with Nicci and Linda, their sons found women with whom the mothers connected immediately.

That's also the case with thirty-one-year-old Melissa. She says her relationship with her mother-in-law is wonderful. "I love my mother-in-law. It's almost as though she has always been in my life." And Emily, who is thirty-two, echoes those feelings. "Most people complain about their in-laws. But I'm very lucky to have her."

Unfortunately, sometimes the girlfriend feels that as hard as she tries, she can never be good enough in his mother's eyes. Jenny, who is now twenty-three, has been dating her boyfriend

since high school. Yet to this day, his mother refuses to introduce her as her son's girlfriend. "She introduces me as 'Jenny'
or sometimes as her son's 'friend,' but never as his girlfriend."
Jenny felt even more unacknowledged when the mom arranged
a surprise birthday party for her son and asked his college
roommate, rather than Jenny, whom to invite. "I know the intimate details of her son's life. Yet I had to hear about it from his
roommate. He asked *me* who I thought my boyfriend would
want to invite. She could have asked me directly." To add insult
to injury, the date chosen to celebrate her boyfriend's birthday
was when Jenny was out of town. So she wasn't even on the
guest list.

No girlfriend, and certainly never a fiancée or wife, should
ever be ignored. In Jenny's situation, she had every right to explain how she felt to her boyfriend. By her remaining silent,
and by his not wanting to offend his mom who had gone to
some effort to plan his party, he assumed, incorrectly, that
everything was fine. Since the party was a surprise, he was unaware of the planning. But once the party was held, he should
have questioned whether his girlfriend had been contacted and
how had the date been chosen.

Cultural Differences

Hannah leaned close to her girlfriends to comment on the
good-looking Indian man standing near her at the bar. The
man had noticed her, too, and when a bartender served her a
mojito, he took the opportunity to ask what she was drinking.
The chemistry between them was instantaneous and intense,
and they spent the next several months, in Hannah's words,
"joined at the hip." Her close-knit Italian Catholic family
adored him. When the young man, named Vijay, developed
cancer, underwent surgery, and spent a month recovering in a
hospital, Hannah took care of him. They talked about mar-

riage, her preference in engagement rings, and the difference in their cultures. In his, he explained, the eldest son bore the responsibility of taking care of his parents, and Hannah told him she was "fine with that."

The romance escalated until the arrival of Vijay's mother, who flew in from India to take care of her ailing son. At first Hannah, respectful of his mother's position and culture, refrained from showing affection to her boyfriend. "He told me I couldn't sit on the bed with him, so I sat in a folding chair. But a month into her visit, I found myself sometimes falling asleep next to him and she would cover me with a blanket. It became more informal and I was allowed to sit on the bed. She gave us some private time, which was surprising to me, and I felt uncomfortable. I didn't want to cross the line and be disrespectful, but Vijay said it would be okay."

Hannah chauffeured his mother on her errands, and she, in return, cooked Hannah dinner. "She wouldn't let me do anything to help in the apartment. She'd say, 'You worked all day, so just eat and relax.'" On Mother's Day, Hannah introduced Vijay's mom to her family. "It was a wonderful day. She got along with everybody. After that, I thought, *This is probably it then.* My boyfriend and I were surprised at how smooth things were going. It was just very easy. Or so I thought."

Trouble erupted a few days later when a cousin of Vijay's called off his wedding. "That's when everything went sour. Because the woman happened to be Italian, like me, his mother got scared. She said, 'I don't want this happening to my son. If this can happen to my nephew, Hannah can definitely do this to my son.'" She immediately forbade her son from seeing Hannah, checking his cell phone to make sure they weren't communicating behind her back. She tried to pressure him to accept an arranged marriage, all the while discrediting Hannah as a possible wife because, as she told her son, she doesn't even cook or clean. She hid the fact that she had repeatedly refused Hannah's offer to help.

Vijay was either unable or unwilling to challenge his influential mom, Hannah says. "I was livid. I said if it were me, I would say, 'Sorry, family, this is my life.' I don't believe she would have given up her only son and disowned him. She had him wrapped around her little finger from day one."

Today Hannah, who has moved to another city to start fresh, tells her own mother that when her little brother starts dating, "I don't care what race or religion the girl is, you never put him through what I went through."

Dr. Lazaroff says mothers act possessive, like Vijay's, believing that marriages have a better chance of succeeding if the husband and wife come from similar cultural, religious, and socioeconomic backgrounds. "The baggage from each side of a family can be very powerful," Lazaroff says. Although this is true, a couple with different backgrounds who stay together over the objections of their respective families can often turn these challenges into a very strong marriage.

When I fell in love with my husband and thought that I would have to choose between him and my family, after a lot of personal and heart-wrenching deliberation I picked him. Because of our difference in religion, nothing we did as a couple could be taken for granted. Every significant issue or event, from our wedding to raising our children, had to be based on compromise and mutual understanding. Consequently, we built our solid marriage on this foundation, and my parents saw that.

Incidentally, the man I married after my first husband died was of the same religion, background, and culture as me. We lasted two and a half years.

Sue says she accepted that her son married a woman from a different religion and race, but was more concerned with her ordinary looks. "I didn't think she was pretty. After I met her, my son asked me, 'Isn't she beautiful?' and I made the biggest mistake. I said, 'She's attractive.' He said, 'You don't think she's pretty. When you say she's attractive, you don't fool me.'" Suitably chastised, a few months later, Sue purposely commented on how beautiful the young woman looked. "Your sons ask you questions because they want you to confirm what they believe. He wanted me to say the woman he was in love with was beautiful. I should have thought it out."

In her son's home now, the couple celebrates all the holidays that center on both of their religions and backgrounds, and Sue is always invited to attend. Her openness and acceptance have resulted in her having an excellent relationship with her son, as well as one with her daughter-in-law.

It's mainly because of a religious difference that Adam feels his mother has not accepted his girlfriend, whom he describes as a stunningly beautiful, intelligent, blue-eyed blonde. "I think if she were Jewish, there would be a different relationship between her and my mom. I really believe it's the religion issue that is the driving force behind any sort of rift between her and my mom. My mom will say she's been my only serious girlfriend and that I should probably date a little more. My theory is that if she were Jewish, my mother would be pushing the marriage card."

Adam's sister also dates a man of a different religion and who dropped out of college. "My mom is feeling that nothing is working out for her kids as she had hoped," he says. "After twenty years the picture she painted looks nothing like she imagined." That's because mothers don't get to paint their children's lives, only provide the canvas. If you expect more than this, you are setting up either yourself or your kids for disappointment and unhappiness.

Sometimes, as with Sue, the boy's mom readily accepts the girlfriend from another religion or race, but the rest of the family is less tolerant. Rebecca experienced this. Although she liked her son's girlfriend despite a difference in religion, she feared telling her ultrareligious father about her. "The rest of my family didn't know my son had a girlfriend because then we would have had to tell them the truth. They probably thought our son was gay. The relationship between my son and my father would be over if he knew whom he was dating."

Her son purposely avoided family get-togethers. But on his grandfather's ninetieth birthday, he had had enough of the charade, and he brought his girlfriend to the celebration. "My dad must have mellowed in his old age," Rebecca says. "He actually was fine with it." Relationships are difficult enough for a couple; they don't need their parents' extended family weighing in.

The problems with religion can sometimes cause a rift even if the families practice the same religion, but with different levels of intensity. Caroline, who is Jewish, says her daughter-in-law was an agnostic, nonpracticing Jew when she started dating her son. But by the time they became engaged, the young woman had turned Orthodox, keeping kosher and refusing to do any work on Saturdays, the Jewish Sabbath. "She suddenly wouldn't ride in a car on a Saturday. She wouldn't open an engagement gift because it arrived on a Saturday. She went from totally nothing to completely *frum* [an extremely devout and observant Orthodox Jew]. My son to this day is not religious, yet they have a kosher, vegetarian home."

In Caroline's situation, it hasn't been just the religious or cultural differences that concern her but differences in the way they each were raised. "My daughter-in-law had no rules in her house growing up. Her parents were free spirits, flower children. They had no boundaries. I think she was seeking some kind of control as she got older, and that's why she sought religion. She's uncomfortable with a lack of perimeters." It's easy for the mom to single out a young woman's different culture or religion as the reason they don't get along. But often that masks other minor differences, as in the case of Caroline's daughter-in-law.

All three of Linda's sons married outside of their religion, and only one converted. "The difference in religion matters," she says, "but I still like my three daughters-in-law." She says she learned how important it was for her to accept them after watching one of her sons be rejected by a former girlfriend's family because of cultural differences. "They were young and it didn't go anywhere, but we were concerned about her family's feelings."

Meg raised all eight of her children in a liberal, Democratic Irish Catholic family. Her one son married into a conservative Republican Italian Catholic family. "So I got them a subscription to *Out of Ireland* magazine," she chuckles. "I buy the grandkids Irish things. It's a dirty trick, but the Italian is so shoved in my face."

Joan can relate to Meg's concerns. She's Italian and married into an Irish family. They go to great lengths to avoid talking to her. "It bothers them that I'm not Irish," she says. "There are a lot of cultural issues. They find lots of way of making bigoted comments; criticism that they pass off as jokes."

I'm not minimizing the significance of a son marrying outside his religion or race and how that could break apart a family. I respect each family's own values. My focus here is how to make sure a mother can remain connected to her grown son and to his wife or girlfriend. She has to recognize that a refusal to accept his choice—for whatever reason—can result in losing him. It's a decision parents must consider deliberately.

Sometimes a relationship between a boy's mother and his significant other is tested not over a difference in religion or race, but over dissimilarity in socioeconomic upbringing. William believes his parents are bothered by the difference in his girlfriend's social status. "I think there's some minor expec-

tation that I would find some nice prep school girl who be-
longs to a country club and plays tennis. I think culturally my
parents have these expectations for me. My mom and dad come
from similar backgrounds to each other. So this is a harder
sell."

In many ways it is. We can convert, and we can learn and
adopt our significant other's culture, but it's impossible to
change our backgrounds. And while this is true, it's really a difference in our core values—and not in our social standing—that
should be the deal breaker. A man can date someone with an
identical upbringing and still be miserable if his idea of a green
bag is the one hanging at the checkout at Whole Foods while
hers is part of the Prada fall collection. If their values are similar, that will transcend any diversity in social upbringing.

Whatever the differences are in race, religion, or culture, a
mother can only do so much. In your case, you may have a son
like Vijay who gives up his girlfriend for his family. Or you
might have a child like me, who would have given up my family
for my husband. Vijay gave up the love of his life. And I—thank
you, Mom and Dad—had the love of mine.

Older, Divorced, and with Kids!

There are two types of cougars, the huge, powerful wildcat and
the woman who dates younger men. Neither one would a mom
want hanging around her son. In fact, many moms may be
more willing to accept a daugher-in-law with a different background than one who could possibly be considered a contemporary.

Yet look at today's culture. It's not unusual to know couples
in which the woman is a lot older than the man. For example,
Demi Moore married Ashton Kutcher, a man fifteen years her
junior, and Susan Sarandon chose Tim Robbins, who is twelve
years younger. In fact, one AARP study shows that 34 percent

of women over forty date younger men. That younger man, say in his late twenties or early thirties, just might be your son.

There are numerous reasons some men prefer older women, they are more self-assured, more sexually secure, and more independent. In fact, they hold a lot of the good qualities that you would seek for your son. However, they also may have been married before and have children, and an ex-husband. And all of them—in one capacity or another—will be entering your son's life, and therefore yours.

In these situations, a mother has a right to ask a few probing questions and possibly even offer some suggestions. For example, you can ask if she has an amicable or contentious relationship with her former husband, and what sort of custody agreement is in place. If there is conflict between her and her ex, your son will be thrust into it. If there is a close relationship, then your son will have to set some boundaries. He may welcome your calm, matter-of-fact constructive comments. "Now that you two are married, you will have to come first in her life, and vice versa. Do you both understand that?" If not, recommend they do some preemptory marriage counseling.

More than likely, the couple understands the problems inherent in a second marriage where one or both have children and an ex-spouse. As in every marriage the rule to follow is to always put your current spouse first. Everything else will fall into its natural place.

Sue still remembers the call she received from her son, telling her he had started to fall for a woman at work who was older and married. "He asked me what to do and I told him to walk away. 'Let her solve her problems with her husband and then you can come into it. She shouldn't leave her husband for you. She should leave because of him.' I don't think he followed my advice."

He didn't. He persisted in seeing the woman, who was eight years older than him and had a seven-year-old child. When

Sue's son admitted to his mother that he had continued dating her and they were hoping to get married after she and her husband divorced. Sue tried to be supportive. "I felt it was his life. I said it would create complications because the boy's father would still be active in his life. He was worried about her having a child, too. I said, 'That's not the problem, because you'll love him and he'll love you.'"

Although initially Sue wished her son had married someone younger and without a child, she acknowledges now that the marriage—which has produced a new baby—has been a happy one. Even when her daughter-in-law's ex-husband shows up at his son's games and birthday parties, everyone is cordial. "I just never imagined my son would have married someone who had been married. A different religion maybe, but not someone who was divorced and with a child."

It's not as though your sons imagine this, either. From the time they begin dating in their teens or twenties they are expecting to marry someone close to them in age who has not been married before. But with so many single moms (ten million live with their under-eighteen-year-old children) and so many divorced women your sons are meeting at work, at clubs, at the gym, it is very possible they will bring home a formerly married woman with a child.

If you are the "older" wife or girlfriend, you know how age has had little negative bearing on your relationship. He's very mature. He is wonderful with your six-year-old daughter. You never had so much in common with any man before. You love each other undeniably. Yet still you feel like "the cradle robber" when you're with his mom. The best way to handle this is with time; time for his mother to see that age makes no difference and time for her to see how much her son loves your child and your child loves him. She'll ultimately forget the age difference and possibly even develop feelings for your child.

One of Meg's sons married an older woman with children,

who became Meg's very first grandchildren. She adores them. "They're great," she says proudly. "I can't imagine my life without them."

> *Who takes the child by the hand, takes the mother by the heart.*
> —Danish proverb

The Girl from Hell

(Mother from Hell to follow!)

As much as I encourage you to accept your son's choice and be supportive, I know there are times you can't. Perhaps the girl is so self-absorbed and spoiled she could make Paris Hilton look like Mother Teresa. It's incumbent on you to help your son see this. The tricky part is making sure her negative attributes are truly destructive, and not just ones you wouldn't have chosen. You have to be objective, shed your maternal prejudices, and view her as a person. Is she really so bad? Is your son miserable? Is it only going to get worse?

Mothers I interviewed who have had one child go through a divorce all say they will never keep their mouths shut again. When I decided to marry my second husband, I know there were family and friends who weren't happy with my decision, but the truth is I wouldn't have heard them at the time. So if your son does go through a divorce, don't blame yourself for not having spoken up. He probably wouldn't have listened to you anyway. However, the fact that you kept quiet gives you a lot more credibility the next time around when he'll probably welcome your opinion.

One of Linda's sons married in his midtwenties but knew two weeks after the wedding that he had made a mistake. His wife, as Linda describes her, was manipulative and ill mannered, and no one in the family liked her. Still, out of respect for her son, Linda said nothing. When the couple soon divorced—the woman fleeing with the china, the crystal, and the sterling silver—her son was crushed. "I made a promise to him that I would never be quiet again if he brought someone home that wasn't right for him," Linda says. In fact, when he later dated another woman whom Linda found to be unrefined and crude, she told him so. He never saw that woman again.

Mothers who choose to involve themselves in their sons' social lives do not have the benefit of hindsight. A difficult girlfriend can, in fact, turn out to be a great wife and daughter-in-law. Once a marriage ends, you will very likely drum up all the faults with this woman and lose sight of what probably attracted your son to her in the first place. She may be inequitably, unquestionably, undoubtedly horrible, but that's because in addition to all of her flaws—ones you might eventually overlook—she's divorced your son.

If your son has ended a bad marriage, he may rebound immediately into another relationship. If he asks your honest opinion about his new girlfriend, still be very selective in what you say. Rather than criticize his choice, if you really have your doubts, encourage him to date, but not rush into marriage.

Dr. Lazaroff counsels, "The mother has to sit down with her son and say, 'Son, I love you. You are special to me and I want the best for you. I want you to have a happy life. I am deeply saddened and distressed that so much anger and rudeness comes from your girlfriend. And I know that you care about her deeply. You need to think about the kind of life you will have if she's capable of this behavior.'"

April's son told her she would really like his new girlfriend because she was an animal lover like herself and had a dog, cat, and potbellied pig. "I asked him, 'Where does the pig sleep?' 'In bed with us,' he replied. I don't know if I was more upset with the fact he slept with a pig or a woman he hardly knew. Then he told us he was in love with her and wanted to get married. He warned me that she had a lot of tattoos, some in places I'd never hear about." When the two women met for the first time, the younger woman was wearing a cardigan sweater to cover her artwork. She asked April if she would mind if she took off her sweater, explaining that she didn't want to embarrass her. "I said, 'Are you comfortable with it? Then I'm okay with it.' So I was prepared. The tattoos went from her shoulder to her wrist, and all I could think was if my son married her she couldn't wear a sleeveless wedding dress."

April remained supportive of this relationship until the woman punched her son in the eye. "When your son shows up with a black eye from his girlfriend, you say, 'Whoa! What did you get yourself into?' I celebrated when they broke up." Years later, when April's son began dating another woman whom she feared might be challenging, too, she merely suggested her son take his time before making a commitment. She was careful not to criticize because she knew her son was falling for this woman.

Today April's son looks back on his earlier relationship and says he appreciates how his mother handled it. "At the time, I was too immature to say, 'Mom, you were right.' She had always been supportive of whomever I had been dating, with the exception of that one woman. Even though my mother was concerned, she made a point to listen to what I was saying first, and then she responded. I was never angry at her."

This is the way to handle your son being involved in a poor relationship. It should not be about the girl, because that will only put him on the defensive. It's about the timing, or the differences, or the potential for problems. Regardless, you have to remain supportive, because to act any other way will make it very difficult for your son to face you when it doesn't work out.

Caroline initially told her son about her concerns but then dropped them when he insisted he was in love. "We were on vacation and taking a long walk on the beach. I said, 'You have to think about getting engaged. She has very different ideas from the way you were raised. You have to decide if you love her enough that these things don't make a difference. And only you can answer that.'" Her son replied that he did love her. "I said, 'You're old enough to know your mind. I'm just here to make sure you're giving a thought to everything.'" Worded carefully, Caroline left room for her son—if he ever needs to—to seek her advice.

Rebecca handled a similar situation the same way. When her son began dating his friend's ex-girlfriend, Rebecca felt the young woman was using him. She didn't have any money and her son took her in. "I never said anything. I just had a feeling. I didn't have any proof. I never let him think I didn't like her, because I didn't want to alienate him." But when he and the woman broke up and then got back together, Rebecca couldn't hold her tongue. "Why would you take her back?" she asked her son. "He said, 'We're trying to work it out.' He finally ended it for good when he found out she was seeing someone else. It didn't hurt my relationship with my son because I said my piece and then he learned on his own. I just prayed that she wouldn't be the one."

A mother should think before she speaks and consider the consequences of what she's about to say. She should never accuse. If she believes her son's wife should be helping out financially but she's too busy playing tennis and going for lunch with her friends, she can suggest the following to her son: "I feel badly that you two are struggling with paying bills. Would it help at all if she were working? Or would the cost of her commute and babysitting be a wash?" Her point is taken.

I asked my son how he would have reacted if I had criticized a former girlfriend with whom he believed he was in love. He said: "I would have been pissed if you had said anything to me about her. I would rather you did what you did, which was not to say anything. Looking back at it, I didn't regret that relationship at all. I feel that at that age—or any age—I should be able to figure out a relationship myself, and not need my mother's help to do so."

But what he also realized is that although I never criticized her or questioned their relationship, I did raise some concerns. "Do you think you can handle her neediness? Do you think you two are on the same page in terms of values?" If he answered, "Yes," I simply said, "Great." If he answered, "No," I just let it go. But I had quietly stated my case.

In fact, when that relationship ended, Noah said to me: "I realized you had noticed the entire time the stuff I hadn't noticed until the end."

The Mother from Hell

Kelly dreads the day she marries her boyfriend and they move in together. Her future mother-in-law has informed her son that she expects to live next door. And that's not even her first choice. What she really wants is her own suite in their home or, barring that, a walk-in closet to hold enough of a wardrobe to cover a lengthy visit. "I look at my boyfriend like, 'Is she serious?' He says no, but then he adds that he doesn't mind her living close to us, just not with us." Small comfort. Having a mother-in-law, whether she's the husband's or the wife's, living next door is a little like being a fish at the aquarium. You can't eat or sleep without all eyes watching.

A former co-worker of mine loved the quaint neighborhood where her son and daughter-in-law lived, so when a nearby house came on the market, she announced she was ready to buy. "No way," commented her daughter-in-law. "You can't live that close." My friend was offended until I reminded her how she would have felt if her mother-in-law had moved next door. "But she was meddlesome and annoying!" she said. Exactly.

What should a wife or girlfriend do if the guy's mother is interfering and overbearing and he fails to do anything about it? Psychologist Lazaroff says, "The wife needs to say to her husband, 'I've tried very hard to be pleasant with your mom and to excuse her rudeness. But nothing has changed and you're allowing me to be a victim of this. We have to decide together how to handle this—either this has to stop forever or only you will have a relationship with her.' It's pretty sad and painful and ugly, especially for the guy and the grandchildren."

Adam's relationship with his long-term girlfriend won't survive his mother living nearby, and he knows it. He says, "It may not cramp my dating style but it may cramp my long-term dating style." If his mother doesn't like a girlfriend, Adam says, it will be very problematic for him. "Your family does play a big role in your relationship, and not getting support from them makes it very difficult to stay with someone."

It's fine for a mother to live near her son and his significant other if that is something *all* the parties want. After my father-in-law died, I insisted my mother-in-law move closer to us. But she was independent and nonintrusive. And honestly, it didn't hurt that she didn't drive.

Marie says her mother-in-law can't hide her negative feelings toward her. "The tension between us is palpable," Marie says. "She's so wildly inappropriate. She can't sit quietly and always wants to make sure she's being heard." At Marie's mother's funeral, her mother-in-law, who is twice divorced, went up to Marie's father and insensitively remarked, "Now we're both single." According to Marie, the tension between her and her mother-in-law worsened after her own mother's death. "My mother-in-law never checked in with me to see how I was doing. I was hurt and angry." So when Thanksgiving came, Marie decided not to include her mother-in-law in the celebration. "She was fit to be tied. How can I keep her son from her? She called her son to say, 'I feel that I'm not being considered. I'm not given the respect I should be as a mother. I hope you feel terrible. Go stew about it and fight with your wife.'"

Marie became so tired of her mother-in-law always complaining to her son that she decided to approach her directly. The outcome: fireworks that keep on exploding. "Right now she's angry and not talking to us. We'll ride this out until she needs a place to go on Christmas. Oh, and she won't exchange Christmas presents this year because she says she has no money. Yet she can't miss a sale at Nordstrom."

Other holidays have proven difficult. On Mother's Day, for example, because her mother-in-law won't acknowledge Marie on this day, Marie refuses to acknowledge her. Her husband now visits his mother alone.

It's understandable how some sons will ultimately go visit their mothers without their wives present. Yet this separation will never help foster a good relationship between the two women. He has to find some way to bring them together—send them to the town's annual flower show, perhaps, or to a local theater production. He may think he's found peace by keeping them apart, but he's only found a cease-fire that can erupt at any moment. The real peace comes when he works at encouraging them to get to know, and like, each other.

Cassie rarely sees her husband's mother anymore. The other woman has made it clear to her son that she prefers to spend time with him, alone. "The only thing that ever happened between us is that I married her son. I took him away from her. He was between jobs when we met and had just moved back home. So now she doesn't seem to like the fact that he's living fifty miles away, and with me," Cassie says. "I used to insist upon going with him to see her, but she just ignored me when we sat around the living room. I also always invited her to our house for the holidays, but she'd complain it was too far to travel. Frankly, it's just as well he sees her by himself."

Cassie's husband could intervene by telling his mother that if she can't learn to accept and like Cassie, then he won't be coming to see her, either. His mother has no just cause to ignore her daughter-in-law. And whether he realizes it or not, he's enabling his mother to continue to treat his wife disrespectfully.

She Loves Me, He Loves Her Not

Fern and her husband loved Greta from the very first time they met. She was sweet and beautiful and obviously very much in love with their son. They included her on their family vacations, invited her parents for their Thanksgiving dinner, and presented her with carefully considered and thoughtful gifts, for which she showed heartfelt appreciation. She eased into the role of the daughter Fern never had. "As the mother of boys, you don't have a daughter so you're always sort of auditioning them. How will they fit into your family? Greta would fit in great." As the young couple's exclusive relationship carried on for two years, Fern began to imagine the phone call announcing their engagement and letting herself indulge in a sneak mental preview of their fairy-tale wedding.

Then her son called. He liked Greta well enough, but he wasn't in love with her. It was over.

Fern and her husband were devastated by the news. "It still hurts today," Fern says. "But you can't pick who your kids are going to marry. I don't know what happened between them and I never asked."

It's not unusual for a mother to become very close to her son's girlfriend only to learn that although the couple's feelings for each other might be over, hers aren't. I adored one of my son's high school girlfriends. She hung out at my house all the time, visited us at the beach, and frequently spent time alone with me. I was disappointed when Noah told me he had ended the relationship.

When I asked my son if he would mind if I continued having email correspondence with her, he seemed indifferent. I took his ambivalence for approval until I realized that if the shoe were on the other foot—if Noah continued a friendship with a man with whom I had, for very personal reasons that would not be shared with my son, broken up—I would be deeply hurt. So I stopped.

As much as you may have liked a son's former girlfriend, it's not your place to continue that relationship. You need to get past it and move on. In fact, once he enters a new relationship, you should sever any remaining ties to his old girlfriend. A new girlfriend should receive your complete attention and not feel that she is competing with a woman your son has already forgotten.

Nicci says one of her son's girlfriends had become part of the family. "She got very close to me, too close," Nicci recalls. When her son began saying that the girl was strangling him with her clinginess, Nicci and her husband "supported him in gently breaking up with her in the right way. Still, it was hard for me when they broke up. We maintained email and phone contact for a while because we both had a difficult time letting go. But we had to move on," Nicci says.

You will always run the risk of getting close to a young woman whose relationship with your son ends. But even when this happens, you've acted properly by being nice and polite to her. When your son enters another relationship, you've shown him that you accept his choices. It also eliminates *your difficult mother* from the equation when they evaluate the reasons their relationship failed.

The possible exception to this is if grandchildren are involved. A man's mother may not want to end her relationship with her ex-daughter-in-law. Each situation is different. If the daughter-in-law has had a particularly contentious breakup with her husband, or perhaps is getting remarried, further complicating all the dynamics, she will probably want no more involvement with her former mother-in-law. A mother must accept this development and expect to see her grandchildren when they are with their dad.

As a widow, when I remarried it was important to both me and to my first mother-in-law, the grandmother of my kids, that we remain close. We did, and she was included in all family functions with my new blended family.

Breakups are never easy, whether you're the one doing it or the one learning about it. But this is between a couple, and parents are here in a supportive role.

The Ex-Games Competition

It's one thing to be compared with a bitchy, spoiled rotten princess. But it's an entirely different matter to be compared with an angelic, charming doll. If your boyfriend's former girlfriend was adored by his family—regardless of what or who caused their breakup—as the new girl on the block, you will become frustrated with their eulogizing the person you've replaced.

Fern's son's new girlfriend wonders if she can successfully compete with the ex-girlfriend, who, in Fern's words, "worked her way into our hearts." She can, but it will take time. Out of respect for this new romance, the ex-girlfriend should no longer be included in Fern's life. If I had continued a relationship with my son's former girlfriend, it would have felt hurtful, if not insulting, to his next girlfriend.

So what can you as the new girlfriend do? You can ask your boyfriend to set some ground rules. He can make it clear to his family that the former girlfriend is part of his dating history and no longer has bearing on his love life. He can insist that his family recognize that that relationship is over. He should remind his mother how she switched hair salons because she didn't like the last highlighting job, and she now enthusiastically embraces her new stylist. She wouldn't want anyone to tell her that her hair looked better before.

Robert says everyone in his family loved his high school girlfriend. "She was great; funny, easygoing, charming, very popular. When it ended, the world came crashing down on me. I had wanted it to end but I was still devastated. I had thought I would be with her the rest of my life but we were just not getting along."

When Robert's next serious girlfriend met his mother, she didn't stand a chance compared with his old flame. "From my perspective, my mom thought she was just okay. She would make comments about the way she behaved. It would upset me that she would say things about my girlfriend."

Counselor Esther Ganz says that some women think a guy's family doesn't like them because they are constantly being compared with a former girlfriend or wife. "This is especially true when the first one passed away. The in-laws loved her, the second one comes in and the in-laws show unreasonable, emotional behavior. In time, they should see how great she is for him. The woman should understand that this comes from an emotional place and fear, and doesn't reflect on her."

It doesn't reflect on her, but that doesn't mean it doesn't affect her. It does, and unfairly so.

Choosing Her Over Family

My parents never realized that they had almost forced me to choose between Charlie and them. They sent off to college a teenage daughter who wore perfectly matched clothes, Weejun loafers, and initial circle pins and who had dated any number of clean-cut guys driving Camaros. What returned home was a hippie in jeans and wire-rims who had fallen in love with a long-haired Vietnam vet who drove a twelve-year-old Volvo. So they were still thinking I would regain my senses and rejoin the family when I announced I was marrying Charlie. What they didn't realize is that I had more control over my senses at that moment than at any point in my life, and I had found my soul mate.

No one—not the family, nor the girlfriend—should ever force a man to give up the people he loves most in the world for each other. It's a no-win—for everyone.

Counselor Ganz experienced this personally. A relative of hers severed ties with his entire family because his wife gave him an ultimatum and he chose her. "When you're abused like that emotionally, you don't realize you have more power than you have," she says. "You give up a situation you could have changed. Now you have no family relationship because of her."

Ganz says that there is usually a pattern among men who acquiesce to their partners and dismiss their families. "This sort of man gives up a lot of his control in general. He's willing to give up his family so he's willing to give up everything. He shouldn't lose his value system over this relationship. He should take a stance with everybody involved.

"I definitely think that many situations are workable," Ganz adds. "People get stuck on old patterns. Here's this new person and new pattern and we have to change them. That takes time with some people, but eventually they wake up and realize they don't want to lose their loved one."

According to Dr. Lazaroff, if none of the parties involved works on this problem, then it becomes a fait accompli. "It's just the way it is," she says. "A man might say, 'My mother doesn't like my wife and my wife doesn't like my mother. So I'll go see my family by myself.' It's pivotal [for] the men to let each side know that it pains him that the people he loves most aren't doing well together, and he feels as though there's nothing he can do."

Peaceful Coexistence

Much in the way a family's standard poodle and Persian cat learn to coexist by recognizing their boundaries, mothers-in-laws and daughters-in-law, whether potential or current, need to do the same. It may take some disagreements, some staking out of territory, some reassurance from their master that they are loved, but they're smart enough to know who eats out of the bowl marked FIDO and who gets the one labeled GARFIELD.

The truth is that once mothers and their sons' girlfriends exhaust all their attempts of vying for position and the attentions of the guy, they realize it's so much less stressful to just try to get along. I'm not telling you to love each other (yet) but, for the sake of not only your son/boyfriend but also your own happiness, discover a peaceful coexistence.

In Lily's case, time has helped her adjust to accepting her son and his girlfriend's relationship. She never assumed the girlfriend her son found in high school would still be with him several years later, so she hadn't initially invested in a relationship with her. Lily says, "I get along with her well now, but it was harder in the beginning. As the kids have grown up, we've reached a comfort level that is mature and reasoned. And I truly believe that she really cares about him."

Sufficient time to adjust might be all a mother and a girlfriend need in order to get along. As well as they both know the man, the two women are strangers to each other. They need patience to learn the other one's quirks and personality, and wisdom to understand how to relate.

Some moms know instinctively that in order to have a good relationship with their son's significant other, they have to treat her like one of their own. This is especially true if the mother has a daughter. Amy realizes that if she overtly favors her two daughters, her son's new wife will further estrange herself from her husband's family. So Amy sat them all down and said, "I want all of us to know we're kind of in this together. I want a relationship with Sandy. She has a mom, and I have daughters. I want to do for her like I do for my own daughters. I don't want a distinction there. There are glitches in the road but I want her to be family. That's my goal."

Has it worked? In the last few months since her son and Sandy got married, Amy is more accepting of their differences, and she's also made a point not to interfere in her and her son's lives. Ironically, she learned this from her own mother-in-law, the woman she didn't speak to for a decade. "Even during that time, my mother-in-law never interfered. And that has made it so much easier to resume a relationship with her now," says Amy.

Caroline has adopted the same approach with her daughter-in-law. When she buys something for her daughter, she buys something for her daughter-in-law, too. "As far as I'm concerned they are both my girls and I treat them equally financially. If she needs me, I run up there the same way I run to my daughter."

Considering your daughter-in-law as an equal in your family means that, just as you do with your own children, you excuse and respect her differences—she sleeps in, you're on the treadmill at dawn. It isn't necessary to become best friends, but it is necessary to be friendly. Sue has learned this now. She wasn't happy when her son became engaged to an older divorced woman with a child, but in time the two women have gotten closer and have come to develop a very respectful friendship. "I'm not her confidante or best friend, but we're definitely closer," she says.

Of course, all of this means you (whether you're the mom or the daughter-in-law) have to get past all the little annoyances. It can make you a little crazy that she stays up late, or that she keeps a messy home, or puts the peanut butter in the pantry rather than the fridge. She is not going to do things the same way you do. When Cindy helps her daughter-in-law with the dishes, she's not allowed to stack the plates. Cindy says, "She has a fit. She says that if you stack you have to wash the bottom of the plate. It's her house and she wants it that way. In my house, they get stacked. My bottom line is you make my kid happy. I'll do whatever you want."

Consider it an act of diplomacy. If you travel to a country where the women keep their heads covered, you'll respectfully cover yours. If you visit a friend's house where all shoes are left by the door, you'll slip off yours. You do this not because you necessarily agree, but out of respect for their customs. Follow this same rule when you're in the home of your daughter-in-law or mother-in-law.

Caroline even abides by her daughter-in-law's rules when her son's family comes for a visit. She provides kosher, vegetarian food and honors the Sabbath by not turning on the television. "My son's first allegiance is to his wife and I won't put him in a position where he has to choose," she says. "I purposely remove any possible conflict." When she goes to her daughter-in-law's disorganized home, she steps over the clutter on the floor and keeps mum. "I don't just bite my tongue, I swallow it."

Hope, too, finds that although her son's girlfriend is respectful of her, she's not really as affectionate as Hope would like. "But as long as she is to my son, that's most important."

The criterion for the mothers is fairly simple: *Does she make my son happy?* For the girlfriend, it's being recognized as the most important person in the son's life—the position his mom once held. Any wonder why this is such a tough relationship?

Jenny says she's been trying for years to seek out and talk to her boyfriend's mom. But most of their conversations cover nothing more personal than current events or work. Jenny says, "At this point, our relationship is based on mutual respect but not much intimacy. I feel like there is a difference in understanding relationships. I see his mom as being very friendly, but in a very formal sense. I feel like I have tried and I'm good with parents and adults in general. I would love to have a close relationship with her. She isn't all that interested in me as a person."

As lacking as their relationship feels, Jenny says it has gotten much better since she told her boyfriend that he needed to intervene. "There never used to be an interaction—even though most of it today revolves around my boyfriend. But things have improved. We send emails infrequently but even that is something new. And now we have begun exchanging presents. She has definitely warmed since that conversation. I'm content with it for now. I do wish we were closer but I have to respect how she wants to handle this."

This may be the best relationship Jenny and her boyfriend's mother can have. If Jenny's idea of a friendship includes physical affection, and her boyfriend's mother's does not, that's simply a difference in culture or habit and not one that means there can't be genuine fondness between them.

Even Kelly admits her boyfriend's mother is making an attempt to get to know her better. "She buys me things, which shows she's thinking of me. She makes sure she has something I like to eat because I'm picky. She tunes in to what I like and she'll fight with her son if he disagrees with me. She's trying even though every once in a while she makes a comment and my anger comes back." This is a big change for her boyfriend's mom. In the beginning, she had hoped and expected they would break up after the prom, but she now realizes that Kelly may one day become her daughter-in-law. Consequently, she's finally willing to develop her own relationship with Kelly.

Regrettably, in Marie's situation, that's not the case. "At this point," she says, "it's a very well-choreographed dance with my mother-in-law. On birthdays, her son gets a gift and I get a card. Yet we always buy her really nice gifts. She avoids me. She doesn't like to make eye contact with me."

Counselor Ganz says if the women don't get along, as in Marie's case, things will never get better unless there is some outside help. "If there is not some involvement, it will never go away. You need an intervention. It could be through counseling or it could be through the son. If the two women are having a problem and it's not getting better, then he should intervene."

Paul says he's tried this. It's not that his mother and his wife don't get along, but they aren't getting as close as he would like. He'll arrange an outing for them, and then one of them will cancel. When that happens, not only are they not spending the necessary time together, but one of them is offended. Regardless of whether you are the mother or the wife, if you receive an invitation from the other woman, never say you're too busy. If she's reaching out to you, you need to accept.

If a relationship between the two women can improve, then in time there should be less and less need for any intervention on the part of the guy. Everyone has to play a part in this; the mother and the girlfriend have to stop engaging the guy in their problems, and the son has to stop enabling them.

Robert believes that as much as his mother and his girlfriend like each other, sometimes his mother gets upset with his girlfriend—for example, if she can't come to a family dinner because she has to work. "She says something to me, and never to my girlfriend. Sometimes I say, 'This is what she needs to do.' And I defend my girlfriend. Other times, I say, 'I don't agree with her decision, but this is what she wants to do.'" Even better—since his mom and his girlfriend do get along—is for these two women to begin dealing with each other directly, and with kindness.

———

Moms, remember when you overheard your little boy and his friends let fly words like, "Loser! You hit like a girl! I'm not playing with you anymore!" when they were in the street playing baseball? And you went outside with that pitcher of lemonade and homemade chocolate-chip cookies (or in my case the slice-and-bake kind) and said, "Boys, play nice." That's what you need to do now.

Girlfriends and wives, you didn't choose her as a mother, just as she didn't choose you as a daughter. If she rejects you because of your background or your age, give her some time to get to know you. In the end, if she sees your core—the reason her son fell in love with you in the first place—she'll cut through those differences.

And to both women, you can't judge a watermelon by its rind, but you'd be disappointed if you turned down a really sweet one.

Keepsakes

1. Moms: Remember how picky your son was when you gave him peas the first time? He's still picky, particularly when it comes to choosing a mate. That should please you.

2. Differences in culture, religion, or race can create an even stronger marriage because the young couple will take nothing for granted.

3. Older woman with kids: Men see wisdom, self-assurance, and sexual security. Who wouldn't want such a daughter-in-law?

4. A woman who insists a man forsake his family is missing the point. They have a lot to do with who he is. And that is the man you love.

5. There are as many girlfriends and wives from hell as there are moms from hell. Fortunately, there are even more heavenly ones.

CHAPTER FIVE

Brothers and Sisters

In Pittsburgh for an annual business meeting, Ginny decided to spend the weekend with her brother and his wife. She arrived at their home clutching her briefcase, overnight bag, and Brooks Brothers suit jacket, and rang the bell. The door was opened by her sister-in-law, Barb, her long hair loosely fixed in a thick knot, a pair of sweet little gold toe rings glistening on her feet. She held an empty mayonnaise jar filled with an amber liquid.

"What's that?" Ginny asked pointedly, dispensing with the pleasantries she reserved for her professional colleagues and slipping past her brother's wife into the house.

"Urine." Barb replied.

"Is your toilet broken?" Ginny stopped and turned around.

"No," her sister-in-law said. "It's for my garden."

Ginny, a self-described gardener by virtue of having replaced plastic flowers with silk ones, silently questioned how her little brother ended up with Mother Nature.

Given how brothers and sisters are raised in the same household and by the same parents, sometimes their selection of partners is surprising—at least to the other siblings. Ginny's brother, a banker by trade and conservative by nature, fell in love with a liberal-leaning, laid-back tree hugger. And Ginny, despite their being married more than twenty years, never understood the attraction.

Sisters, whether they are older and protective, or younger and reverential, still think they know what's best for their brothers. And if the female he chooses doesn't fit into that image—and frequently, she doesn't—his sister will let him know. Her relationship with her brother is very different from the one he has with their mother. Mothers recognize that as their sons age, the balance in their relationship will shift. It progresses from Mom being fully in control to her son taking charge of his own life. As difficult as it might be to accept this change, mothers are smart enough to know it's natural and inevitable.

A sister, on the other hand, expects aging to have no impact on the relationship between her and her brother. If she always got to ride shotgun with Mom, she probably still intends to. If her older brother used to defend her honor on the school bus, she still counts on that protection. Their relationship doesn't change whether they're downing Jell-O pops or Jell-O shots. And for this reason most sisters can be quite undisguised—maybe too much so—in admitting how they feel about their brother's girlfriend.

> *Our brothers and sisters are there with us from the dawn of our personal stories to the inevitable dusk.*
> —Susan Scarf Merrell, author and journalist

Family Feud

No matter how devoted siblings are as children, if they ultimately dislike each other's significant other, a wedge may be driven between them and, consequently, their entire family.

Cassie fears this could happen to her. Sensitive to sibling rivalry, she has always been proud of how well her children got along. Then her son discovered girls, adding an ingredient to the family that like a misdirected egg yolk in a bowl of meringue, threatened its collapse. It all began when Cassie and her husband invited their son's girlfriend to join them for a long weekend on a lake. Almost immediately the girl voiced her disappointment with the family's choice of restaurants and activities. While Cassie suppressed her annoyance with the young woman, her daughter did no such thing. Instead she took her mother aside and declared, "I don't like that girl!"

"My heart broke," recalls Cassie. "I suddenly understood how this stranger could ruin the wonderful relationship my two kids had since they were little. I told my daughter that she had no choice. She had to like the person her brother loved. 'No, Mom,' she told me. 'Maybe you do, but I don't.'"

With that pronouncement, Cassie began to imagine the holidays that would no longer include her son because he'd choose to go to his wife's house where—even if he didn't feel more comfortable—she certainly did. While Cassie realized that in order to keep her son in her life, she had to get along with his girlfriend, her daughter felt no such obligation.

According to Dr. Lazaroff, "The reason sisters have trouble with their brother's girlfriend is that they see him as their buddy. This other female is taking away their brother and she'd better be good enough for him." Unfortunately, sisters all too often don't think she is. And while Mom just might hold the same opinion, she isn't about to sacrifice her relationship with her son by giving it.

Sons also know that even if they become involved with someone their mothers don't particularly like, Mom will always be there. Adult sisters, though, can be entirely less forgiving. They will stop communicating with their brother over a snub on a birthday or a rivalry over finances; add to that a dislike for a brother's spouse, and you have a relationship that's—if not over—then placed in indefinite hibernation.

The dynamics in Sharon's family haven't been the same since her brother got married. "I never liked her," confesses Sharon, the eldest of five. "Whenever she was in the room she was the center of attention. She was high-maintenance. My brother didn't know I felt this way because I always acted nice and supportive. I would talk to her and try to make her feel welcome. But over time, she began to say things that made it impossible to remain friendly."

Among those comments was criticism for the way Sharon's parents babysat her daughter. " 'Those two parents raised your husband,' I told her. 'So what does that say about your husband? You have to have respect for my parents, and until you do, I can't have a relationship with you.' I told my family that I was done. I wanted nothing to do with her until she started to show respect for my parents."

As happens with a lot of families, financial matters caused the situation to further deteriorate. The sister-in-law, who reaped the monetary rewards of her husband's claim in the family business, complained about his work hours and insisted her father-in-law work longer. She also refused to sign an IOU when her in-laws loaned them money to buy a house. "She became a lightning rod in our family. When the business ended, they moved back to Florida where she grew up. It's pretty clear that she didn't want to be with my family. She intentionally put a wedge between us and my brother," says Sharon, who now sees her brother only when he comes home alone for special occasions, and hasn't spoken to her sister-in-law in eight years. "I think of her as a witch who put a spell on him," she adds. "My brother always took his wife's side, which over the years has made me wonder whether she was just his mouthpiece. It was hard for me to believe that he would sit by and let her treat the family the way she did unless he was complicit with her views."

It's easy for a sister to dislike the person a brother has chosen, especially if she drives him away from his family, but if her brother is content, a sister needs to consider the reasons why. He obviously sees something intrinsically good in his wife or girl-friend, and although for a mother, who wants peace at all costs or at least an occasional phone call from her son, that's often enough, for a sister it's not. Even if she's willing to recognize the positive attributes of this woman, she still expects her relation-ship with her brother to remain unchanged. But in reality, once another woman enters his life, their relationship will not be the same whether she was the older sister he deferred to or the younger one he catered to. Change, by the way, doesn't have to be for the worse. It may mean a relationship now built more on an adult friendship and less on sibling birth-order roles.

If it is impossible to like this woman, as in Sharon's case, then a sister could try to maintain a separate relationship with her brother, speaking to him on his cell phone or at work. But Lazaroff warns, "This is really hard on the guy, and is felt by the entire family." No matter what, the sister should refrain from disparaging this other woman, as tempting as that may be. In-stead, she should express her concerns about her brother. "You never used to be this stressed. What happened?" Or, "Do you feel you can resolve your financial problems?" Or, "Do you ever regret the career path you've chosen? It's so different from the one you talked about when we were younger." The conse-quence of this is that a sister can remain a safe haven for her brother. If his relationship with his significant other lasts for-ever, the sister still has her brother. If it doesn't, she hasn't made it difficult for him to trust her again.

And Daughter-in-Law Makes Two

Truth be told, I really got along with my mother-in-law because there was no competition for her attention. She had no daughters, or other daughters-in-law for that matter. She could give me a gift, spend time with my kids, and make my favorite foods, all without feeling she was slighting anyone else. It's different when a brother has a sister. His girlfriend may feel she has to compete with his sister for his mother's attention, or she may feel insignificant and unwelcome because the mother favors her daughter.

The mother, for her part, must maintain a balancing act, simultaneously convincing her daughter that she'll always come first and her daughter-in-law that she plays no favorites. This task is rendered more challenging when the brother's sister doesn't like his significant other.

Joan thinks her mother-in-law likes her even though she behaves as though she doesn't when in the presence of her daughters. "If we're meeting one-on-one, she's cordial, but if she's meeting me in front of her daughters, you can tell she acts differently."

I dated a guy whose mother also did that. When her daughter was present, the mom refused to address me, instead directing conversations to her daughter and son. On the couple of occasions when she and I were alone, she treated me differently, actually acting friendly and interested. But as soon as her daughter reappeared, I went back to being invisible. Once, the change in her was so abrupt, I couldn't believe she didn't see it. We were sitting at her son's kitchen table and I offered to make her a cup of coffee. She accepted, rather pleasantly, but just as I was pouring the coffee into her mug, her daughter arrived. The mom jerked the mug away as though its filling up with coffee created a secret, intimate bond between us, like two kids on a playground becoming blood sisters. The coffee went everywhere, and I was left cleaning it up while the other two women retired to the living room. I knew then that as hard as I tried with this mother, her daughter would always stand in the way.

If you're the wife or girlfriend, it helps to accept the possibility that you may never be as close to a mother-in-law as her own daughter is. But just because a woman's daughter won't let you come between them, it doesn't mean they both don't like you—dare I say, love you. You need to accept your second-place position with grace. That takes pressure off the mother and doesn't threaten the daughter, and allows you to have a meaningful relationship with both women. If, however, the sister remains standoffish, then work on that relationship first. If you get along with your boyfriend's sister, his mother will naturally follow. That doesn't necessarily work in the reverse.

If you're the mother and you sense competition between your daughter and current or future daughter-in-law, treat them as you would two siblings. Be caring and respectful to both. If you want to provide more to your daughter, then do it privately. If your son's girlfriend has a mom, she's probably being treated well by her. But if, for example, you give out Christmas or Hanukkah presents in the presence of both women, try to give comparable gifts. Your daughter will be fine with it, and your son's significant other will be grateful.

If Nicci has any concerns about her son's serious girlfriend, it's not with her but with her own daughter's reaction. Nicci senses an undercurrent of jealousy when she tells her daughter that she is meeting her son's girlfriend to go shopping or have lunch. "My older daughter is very close with me so I've noticed that she wasn't so quick to embrace the girlfriend. Nothing overt, maybe not even anything that my son and his girlfriend would notice, but I noticed. The two women have opposite personalities. I do think part of it is the whole notion of sharing me with someone else—with another girl who will be family."

Nicci has also found that the speed in which her son and his girlfriend's relationship developed didn't bother her as much as it did his sister. Moms like Nicci have already been experiencing a change in their relationship with their growing sons, so the existence of a serious girlfriend helps to explain it. If they like the girl, they are okay with the relationship progressing. Sisters, who may already be living apart from their brothers whether for college or for work, may have fewer opportunities to get to know this other woman. She remains a stranger to them, and therefore, they deduce, to their brother.

Nicci says that although she accepts her son falling in love and moving in with his girlfriend, his older sister does not. "I'm cool with it," Nicci says. "But to my older daughter, it became 'Whoa! All of a sudden they're living together, and she's with our family.' I don't think my daughter had enough time to adjust." Interestingly, Nicci's not as close with another daughter who—feeling no competition for her mother's attention—readily accepted her brother's girlfriend.

Twenty-four-year-old Nonnie empathetically relates to how out of place the girlfriend of Nicci's son must feel. Her boyfriend's sister is so close to her mother, they speak as frequently as four times a day. Nonnie, on the other hand, describes her relationship with her own mother as fractured and, consequently, has sought out her boyfriend's mom. "His mom is easy to talk to and very accepting of my friends. They come over to her house to hang out, and she gives them advice about boys." There is a degree of separation that allows a boy's mother to connect with his girlfriend differently from how she connects with her own daughter. This is one of those positive sides I mentioned earlier. If you have a daughter, you know that if you sat around your kitchen table chatting with her friends and passing along advice about guys, your daughter would most likely be mortified. And even though a daughter would reject this sort of "girl talk" with her mother present, she may feel resentful if it goes on with her brother's girlfriend. Nonnie says, "The only thing I could imagine causing tension between me and his sister is if she feels I'm in a close relationship with her mother."

It is a normal reaction for daughters who love their mothers not to want to share them, especially with someone who isn't family. And if this young woman happens to be somewhat distant from her own mother, she poses an even greater threat to his sister. Both Nonnie and Janet compensate for poor relationships with their own mothers by becoming close to their current or future mothers-in-law, and this agitates their sisters-in-law.

In Janet's case, she's tried to befriend her three frosty sisters-in-law who resent her "very good" relationship with their mother. "My sisters-in-law don't appreciate their mother. They'll say to me, 'You didn't grow up in that house. You didn't know how hard it was with her.'" Actually, Janet does. She thinks the same about her own mother, which is what drives her to having loving feelings toward her husband's mom. And so long as the sisters aren't around, the feelings have been mutual. When the sisters are present, Janet is reminded that she's related by marriage only. "She will have her three daughters do things with her, and then she'll do things with her other daughter-in-law and me, together. It's times like those I feel less like a daughter and more like a daughter-in-law. It hurts me."

I know how she feels. I think twice before pouring a cup of coffee.

Try as She Might, She Just Doesn't Fit In

It's not just that Janet is irritatingly close to their mother, it's also that, in their opinion, she doesn't fit in. "I came from a different background," she says, "so they look down on me. They wanted their brother with another princess like themselves. It's clear I'm not who they would have chosen for him."

Since you are often not who his mother or sister would have chosen, no matter how hard you try to blend in, you'll always feel a bit like the interloper. To lessen this reaction, when you're in your boyfriend's family's home, even if you disapprove of their habits or practices, follow along. If, for instance, they like to leave the television on during dinner, tolerate the noise, knowing you can shut it off when you're in your own home. Dr. Lazaroff says, "If the girlfriend wants to fit in, she has no choice but to do things the way his family does when she's with them."

More often than not, it's not just a difference in customs that makes you feel like an outsider, but a genuine difference in who you are. Like twenty-three-year-old Jenny, you may "stick out" when you're with your boyfriend's family because your interests and personality—or more acutely, your race or religion—differ from theirs. Jenny, in particular, doesn't relate well to her boyfriend's sisters, one of whom is athletic and the other social. "I fall in between the two," she says. So when Jenny tries to fit in, she senses a reserved but cold response from the sisters. Unfortunately, she may not be wrong. To hear one of these sisters speak, "Jenny on paper is great. What's wrong with the girl? It's not that she's not smart, not motivated, not polite, because she is. But there is a difference in backgrounds [religious and economic, in her case]. My parents are a lot different than hers."

The mother of Jenny's boyfriend resigns herself to the fact that her daughters are unaccepting. When her son once said that Jenny didn't feel welcomed in their home, she told him, "'That's not something I would intentionally do. But I can't control your siblings.' The girls notice everything—degrees of warmth, openness. But the truth is I don't know who my son would bring home who would be a slam dunk with his sisters."

Precisely. Sisters don't expect their family standing and their relationships to ever change, so any woman a brother introduces might feel as welcomed as a hangover after a night on the town. A sister knows it's inevitable, but that doesn't make the headache go away. Sometimes the most a girlfriend can expect from her boyfriend's sister is cordiality and occasional inclusion. Understanding and appreciation for her difficult position in the family may be too much to ask. Joan says she recognizes that her large family can overwhelm her brothers' wives. "We're so big and opinionated and we're a little more closed than we should be," she says. "It's hard for someone with a shy personality to move into our family." Joan appreciates her sisters-in-law's discomfort because she knows firsthand how it feels to be ostracized by a husband's family. "I know how uncomfortable it is to fit into a close-knit family. I'm definitely the odd person out with my husband's sisters. So I like to think I'm a little more sensitive to that when it comes to my brothers' wives."

As with Janet, Joan's relationship with her mother-in-law is actually better than the one she has with her husband's sisters. "I think, generally speaking, my mother-in-law likes me even though she doesn't like what I represent. You can see this dissonance come over her. What's happening here. We're not supposed to like her. She's a Democrat. She's from the South. But the main culprits are—and always have been—his sisters."

Over the years Joan has learned to hold her tongue and defer to these women, not just because they are older than her, but also because to do otherwise would cause unrest. She says, "There is no obvious anger because that would be real and we avoid authenticity at all costs. That would actually be refreshing. I would like to get it out there. I'd rather take the hit directly. They bully you. It's a form of domestic harassment."

Sisters are also very likely to complain directly to their brother, who would just as soon take no action rather than embroil his wife or girlfriend in a tiff with his sibling. Most girlfriends, though, would prefer to face the other woman head-on. As Janet says, "I can fight my own battles."

Sometimes even a welcoming sister-in-law can be unintentionally exclusive. Just reminiscing about family history naturally leaves out a brother's girlfriend. Joan says, "If you're sitting about talking about childhood and you're the in-law, you sit there with nothing to add, no insights. You're excluded. No one is trying to be malicious but the results are the same."

So what can you do as the wife or girlfriend? You can't force his sister to like you, but you can help everyone else—especially your husband—to see that you're trying. Invite her to a girls' night out. Plan some time alone with her. But most important, always speak lovingly of her brother. For example, don't call him moody (she can, you can't) or cheap (she'll think you're a gold digger). Don't take the bait if she criticizes him. Defend him, and never confide in her about your relationship difficulties. If she feels she can trust you with her brother, she will ultimately think you're not so bad. And honestly, in some cases, that's pretty good.

The mother of Jenny's boyfriend encourages her daughters to accept Jenny. "I tell them, 'You don't have a choice. If the tables were turned and you brought home someone, I would expect your brother to accept him. This has been a long relationship. From the time they started dating, she's not the same person, and you're not the same person. You got off on the wrong foot. You need to find a way to start over.'"

Fortunately, not all sister-in-law relationships are tense. In fact, many women develop rich and strong connections and actually consider themselves to be sisters. Regardless of whether you're the sister or the brother's significant other, you should try to look at the other woman as someone you might meet at a party, or at work, whose company you enjoy. You could end up with a new and wonderful friend, bound not just by a handful of common interests but also by a mutual love.

"You want the whole thing to work," adds the mom of Jenny's boyfriend. "You want the girlfriend and the sisters to like each other. They don't have to adore each other but they have to like each other."

> *Sibling relationships—and 80 percent of Americans have at least one—outlast marriages, survive the deaths of parents, resurface after quarrels that would sink any friendship. They flourish in a thousand incarnations of closeness and distance, warmth, loyalty and distrust.*
> —Erica E. Goode, in "The Secret World of Siblings,"
> *U.S. News & World Report,* 1994

Brothers and Sisters: The Glue That Bonds Them

The greater the bond between a sister and brother, the more threatened by or critical of his significant other the sister might be. She'll see things to which his mother will either be oblivious or purposely turn a blind eye. And unlike the mother, she's likely familiar with the music the girlfriend listens to, the clubs she visits, the people she hangs out with—and from that will form a judgment about her. Her brother need say nothing.

A sister's relationship with her brother is unique because, although they are family, they are also friends and contemporaries. And while we expect to be on equal footing with a friend, a sister expects that and more from a brother's girlfriend. She wants this other female not only to fit the high standards she has for her brother, but also to show just the right amount of reverence to her.

Lazaroff says, "Sisters show more judgment and pickiness than do the boys' mothers. They think, *Can that person take my place and do a good enough job as a friend for my brother?* And, *Will I be booted out?*"

Sisters aren't necessarily going to be "booted out" of their brothers' lives, but they do have to accept someone who will be closer to their brother than they have always been. It's a matter of moving over to give this other woman—and her brother—space. That's not the same as the mothers, who literally have to give up first place when their son falls for a woman. Sisters simply have to make room.

"I adore my brother so I think any girl would be lucky to have him," says Candace, who finds it impossible to accept her older brother's girlfriend despite the fact they've been dating for more than five years. Candace says the three of them have the same group of friends, which adds additional pressure to her relationship with his girlfriend. "His girlfriend is the one thing we disagree on. Though never openly."

That's fortunate. A sister unreservedly criticizing her brother's girlfriend will initially harm her relationship with him. Not unlike with his mother, he wants to feel he has his sister's support so that if he ever needs to confide in her, he can do so without hearing her opinion. He can tell his sister more than he can his mom because he relates to her as an equal, a peer.

On the positive side, unlike moms, whose negative comments about a son's significant other can endure, sisters have a little more leeway with an occasional critical remark (constructive ones, not unkind comments aimed at the girlfriend). A brother knows that friends, which is how he hopes to perceive his sister and girlfriend, often disagree, make hurtful comments, and then make up.

Every time my son had a change in his life regarding girlfriends—when he broke up with someone, and when he met another—he called his sister, Debra, first. She'd run interference by calling me to say, "Mom, Noah has something to tell you. Don't be upset with him." By now I know that if my daughter's not upset with her brother, I probably won't be, either. When the phone rings again I know it's my son calling to break the already-broken news. Frankly, I love that my kids are so close. But then I'm their mother, not the significant other of either one of them.

Candace says she talks to her brother about almost everything but the seriousness of his relationship with his girlfriend. "I haven't had a heart-to-heart about her with him. I think that she knows how close we are and that she wouldn't say anything about me to him. I'm kind of off limits to her and she is with me in talking to him. We don't discuss marriage. If it's going to happen, it's because she wants it to."

Twenty-seven-year-old Laura says she and her younger brother, whom she considers her best friend, often comment on each other's significant others, and not necessarily positively. "He'd want to know things like why his girlfriend is always mad at him. I'd tell him she was looking for attention. I'd say, 'This isn't fair to you. You are choosing to stay in an unhealthy relationship. You keep going back to her.' He never said he minded my advice. Sometimes he would say, 'Yeah, yeah, yeah,' and he'd take from the conversation what he wanted to take. But he always came back. He never stopped talking to me. We do tell each other the truth, and we're pretty brutal sometimes about relationships. But I listen to him about my boyfriends, too. He always ends up being right. I broke up with my last year's relationship because he was a jerk to my brother."

While sisters can be more critical than a mother, they also tend to relate better, especially since they've been in relationships themselves. As Laura says, "I've been there. I've had the bad boyfriends. I know what it's like to have the boyfriend nobody likes." She initially liked her brother's girlfriend until, as she says, "she turned psycho. I think she was a little bit threatened by how close my brother and I were."

Even when a brother and sister are close, most guys will drop their sister—at least for a time—if she forces him to question his romance. A brother will accept that his sister may not particularly like his girlfriend and that she cares about him. But if she repeatedly harps on the detrimental aspects of a girlfriend, he'll shut down.

Caroline knows that although her two children are very close, sharing similar ethics, morals, and mutual respect, there is a limit to how much her daughter can say. "They've always been supportive of each other," Caroline says. "She decked someone for him when she was ten and he was thirteen. It was a girl and he couldn't hit her, so my daughter did it for him. Nobody messes with her brother." But now that her brother is married, he refuses to hear what his sister thinks. "This is the first time he has ever said, 'Don't go there,'" Caroline says.

So Much for Brotherly Love

I met four girlfriends for dinner, and the conversation turned to family estrangements. Of the five of us, one had two children who didn't speak to each other; another didn't speak to her brother; and one woman didn't speak to her sister, while her husband didn't speak to his brother, and her son didn't speak to any of his in-laws. The basis for all the discord was either money or spouses. While we've been talking about the closeness between a brother and sister, sometimes none exists. And in an odd way, the sibling's significant other could possibly bridge the gap. At any rate, she probably can't make it any worse.

Hope's two kids, a twenty-seven-year-old son and thirty-two-year-old daughter, have different passions and dispositions: Her son is conservative and focuses on making money; her daughter is liberal and involved in social causes. Not surprisingly, her son chose for his wife someone like himself. She likes clothes and jewelry and emphasizes physical appearance, while the sister is more earthy and athletic. Despite the differences, because the sister poses no threat to the brother's relationship, the two women sincerely like each other. And in fact, Hope says, "My kids are closer today than they were when they were younger because the two women get along."

Janet wishes she could have this sort of friendship with her husband's sisters, who weren't all that close with her husband when they were kids. "His older sister ruled the roost. She still has major control issues and has no intention of letting go no matter how friendly I might try to be."

Unfortunately, money always complicates family issues, as it has in Janet's and Sharon's situations. When a family business is involved and the sisters see their sister-in-law directly benefiting from her husband's role in it, they can be unrelenting in their animosity. Janet's oldest sister-in-law resents her brother's involvement in the business. "He was told from the day he was born that he'd be taking over the business," Janet says. "His older sister has always felt it should be her."

It's understandable that when there is such competition, each woman may feel justified in her dislike for the other. So long as Janet directly benefits from her husband's job, as hard as she tries, she will never develop a good relationship with her sister-in-law.

Brother and Sister Grow Up

A sister who doesn't get along with her brother's wife or girl-friend has a few choices: She can cut off all ties, she can include and accept the woman, or she can try to maintain a separate, even secretive, relationship with her brother.

In Candace's case, she now sees her brother by himself. "He and his girlfriend do their own thing and we do our own thing. If that's how it has to be, then so be it." She goes to great lengths not to mention his girlfriend when they're together, and intentionally appears ambivalent when he mentions her name. "I don't ask him about her. The other day I dropped him off at his apartment and he invited me to join him for dinner. I asked him who was going to be there and he said his girlfriend. I said, 'Oh cool.' He could sense something and said, 'You're going to be nice to her tonight. Right?' That was unusual for him to put it out there. My mom said I should talk to him. I have to make sure it's in a constructive, nonconfrontational I-care-about-you kind of way. Because when it comes to her, he isn't himself. He defers to her, explaining how 'She only does that because you do this . . .'"

In Candace's opinion, she believes her brother has changed to suit his girlfriend. He probably has. When we enter a relationship, we develop interests closer to those of our significant other; consequently, the people who knew us before, whether they are our family or friends, may feel confused or left out. "He'll do things with her that he wouldn't normally do, like tour a historical site," says Candace. "His interests change for her. That bugs me. He doesn't want to do that. He's changing to fit her. He's complacent, almost to his detriment, and she has his whole life planned for both of them." The point here is that this is probably what her brother wants, too.

A sister should expect that when her brother falls in love—even if it's with someone she likes—their relationship will change. It's part of the maturation process he needs to go through, and rather than being the older brother or the little brother, his new position of lover, boyfriend, or husband will be his priority. This is the way it should be, and the sooner a sister realizes this, the sooner she can get to know and appreciate her brother as a grown-up.

Laura sees a change in her relationship with her younger brother. "I think that as we are getting older, he is pulling away a little bit more when it comes to girls. Guys talk differently, anyway. They keep it more separate. We used to talk about everything. 'Do you like her? Do you think she's pretty?' But as soon as the girls had the potential to be in a serious relationship with him, he stopped discussing them with me."

She's beginning to accept this development in her relationship with her brother. "I need to stop looking at people like they are for me," she acknowledges. "If he truly loved her and said she was the one for him, I would accept that. At least, I would like to think I would. I would hope that I would."

Malcolm in the Middle, Again

Even Candace admits that her brother recognizes the tension between her and his girlfriend and that he is at a loss as to what to do about it. He confesses that he hasn't helped the situation by keeping his girlfriend and his sister apart. "I created an either-or thing, which was bad, and that hasn't repaired itself," he says. He appreciates that Candace says little about the girlfriend because he's afraid if he discusses either woman with the other, he'll be "stirring a pot that is better left untouched." He believes that his girlfriend would like to get along with his sister but feels intimidated by her. "She doesn't think she's as cool as my sister and [thinks] my sister doesn't respect her. What can you do? It's met with total indifference anyway," he says. "Nothing I'm going to say will change the way things are."

Lodged in the middle between two discontented women is a guy's worst nightmare. He doesn't hold the same power to induce guilt over his sister that he does over his mother, yet he can't control her feelings, either. The most he can hope for is civility, and to that end he can and should speak to both women.

He can say the following to his sister: "This is it. I love this woman and expect to be with her for life. I love you, too, and always will, but I won't give her up for anyone." (Sisters need to hear this if they are still thinking this relationship isn't going to last. And if they don't like the girl, they probably are thinking this.) "I can't force you to like her, but I can ask you to see how happy she makes me. If I see you happy in a relationship, no matter what I think of the guy, I'll do my best to be friendly. Our relationship means too much to me."

If we love our brothers, we should understand this.

Candace's brother says, "There were many times when I felt I didn't deserve this. These are two likable people who have no reason not to get along. And they both expect me to provide the solution. In fairness, I should have played a bigger role than I did. I definitely know that my girlfriend would put the onus on me to solve the problem, and I felt powerless. I didn't know what to do to fix the problem. I had two upset parties on either side with nowhere to go."

Now, after years of trying to work it out, he's given up. "They've never been close and I don't know if they ever will be. That gets to me sometimes, but I've learned to just accept it. It's not my problem and it doesn't affect me that much. It's not worth dealing with, frankly."

I realize the way Candace's brother feels is how most brothers feel. They want their sister and significant other to get along, but if they can't achieve some type of friendship between them, then they'll stop trying. When I asked Noah how he perceives his sister's relationship with his girlfriends, he says, "Debra has always been supportive of any relationship I had. I feel that she tries to do her best to like all of the girls." Yet when an incident came up involving one of them, he was annoyed that she complained to me and not to him. "That irked me," he says. "I wish she would have said something to me. I would have talked to my girlfriend, who would have apologized directly to Debra. All my girlfriends have wanted to have a relationship with her because they know how close we are."

Adam, whose biggest conflict with his girlfriend has come from his mother and even his younger brother, says it's his sister who has been the most supportive. His sister has no intention of losing her brother over a relationship. And she has reached out not only to him, but also to his girlfriend.

"A sister has to look at the possible consequences and take a look at her own behavior," says counselor Ganz. "She may be trying to hold on to her brother. The sister doesn't have to be forced to like the girlfriend, but she does have to be nice to her. The motivation is not to lose her brother. Maybe he has to say to his sister, 'It hurts me. I love both of you, but this is going to be my permanent relationship.' Doing nothing to rectify the situation is terrible."

Going Around Malcolm

Betty has never liked her sister-in-law, but she is cordial to her because her brother loves her. "My brother married a girl that I would have never picked for him in a million years—different class, different religion, different beliefs. I care about her because my brother loves her, but I would never, ever pick her for a friend. She's boring as hell. I talk to my brother every week and I see him a couple times a year. I'm gracious and lovely when she's here. If I call their house, she gives the phone to my brother. She doesn't want to talk to me, either."

But Betty says she's pleasant to the other woman because her brother is satisfied. "He adores this woman. Even if I see her as not educated, not attractive—I could go on and on—she loves their children. What I look for is that he's happy and he has someone who will care for him when he's ill, care for his kids, be a financial partner. She's not at all a burden on him." If this is the best sisters can hope for, then that's plenty.

Candace admits she hasn't taken the time to really get to know her brother's serious girlfriend and has always kept a distance. She feels it's mutual, though, saying that she makes no attempt to be part of her family. She comes over, converses briefly with her mother, says hi to her father, and then goes off with her brother. "In five years I have never given her a hug, which is weird for me, since I hug everyone. I am certainly to blame for a lot of it," Candace admits. "I was so young that I don't remember their relationship starting and all of a sudden there's my brother with a serious girlfriend. I want him to have a girlfriend who invites me out to lunch, who wants to get close to me—for me. But I think I've gotten to a point of giving up."

She shouldn't give up. If the girlfriend doesn't take the initiative, then Candace should. Don't stand on ceremony, and don't rely on the guy to create situations that bring you two together. They won't. It's easier for them to keep you apart than to hear negative remarks about the other. So take the initiative, whichever role you're in.

Candace's mother tells her daughter to learn how to make this girl important to her, since she's important to her brother. "I think to myself, *You're just the girlfriend. I'm family. I'm not getting kicked out. I have nothing to lose.* But my mom says, 'You have your brother to lose.'" So true. Sisters need to decide what's important to them: having a relationship with a brother who has a girlfriend they can't stand—or having no relationship with either of them.

Jenny says she doesn't have a relationship with her boyfriend's sister, and has always suspected she doesn't like her. "We are around the same age. There is the cattiness of being girls. I tried a long time with his sister but never got anywhere. We're in different social circles. We're cordial and friendly. We've never spent any time alone." Imagine if they did. Who knows what could happen?

Robert would love his sister and girlfriend to spend alone time together. They get along well but don't seek each other out unless Robert is around. "I'm hoping for a time when they'll pick up the phone and chat together. My sister calls me on my cell phone but she doesn't ever speak to my girlfriend."

It takes so little effort for either one of these women to call or email the other. Even if she assumes she isn't liked, she may be pleasantly surprised at the welcoming reaction she gets. There is no excuse not to try.

————

A sister who is willing to reject her relationship with her brother because she doesn't like his significant other will over time suffer a painful loss. As we age, we find we need our family even more. "Some people have lost the investment in their family," comments Joan. "There is something wrong when it's easier to get out of a marriage or a sibling relationship than a cell phone contract."

Keepsakes

1. A sister's dislike for her brother's significant other will affect the entire family. It's so much easier to look for her positive points. Try this one: She loves your brother.
2. Moms should recognize that daughters may feel slighted by the attention focused on a daughter-in-law. They can rectify the situation by showing impartiality, at least when everyone's together.
3. Sisters should put themselves in the girlfriend's shoes and try to appreciate how awkward it is for an outsider to join a family.
4. If need be, the man, in this case, should definitely intervene between his wife and his sister. He can prevent estrangement.
5. Yes, your brother is wonderful and anyone is truly lucky to have him. But he probably isn't perfect.

CHAPTER SIX

Just When It's (Sort of) Under Control, Other Relatives Join the Fray

Intimidation and insecurity had set in even before I was introduced to the mother of one of Noah's girlfriends. Her daughter had raved about her mom's considerable talents: She had organized several high-society functions; decorated her million-dollar mansion without the aid of a professional (!); sat on any number of local boards, including the ladies' auxiliary of a tony hunt club; and accomplished all of this while helping her nanny raise three children.

Then we met.

We were attending a party at the home of a mutual acquaintance. The girl's mother and I stood across from each other on either side of a scrumptious-looking buffet. I tried desperately to find a place to focus my gaze as she dug her fingers into the cold cuts—meticulously arranged by some caterer in an intricate fish-scale pattern—raised them to her lips, chewed, licked her fingers, and then went back for more.

Her Chanel sheath and diamond-studded Rolex aside (so much for my flea-market copy), this woman, presented to me in absentia as a pillar of refinement and culture, was as ordinary as they come. The problem, though, was that she didn't think so. *She* had the upbringing, of course, to know what was best for her daughter and, by association, my son. And she figured she could teach his less sophisticated mom a few things.

Behind a façade of politeness (I can play the game, too) we conversed about the weather, the fun party, and a shared friend. Despite giving every observer in the room the sense we were fast becoming friends, we obviously held the same first impression: *Like the kid, hate the mother.*

Just when the mother and the girlfriend have figured out how to relate to each other, more relatives join the mix. The introduction of these less involved family members can throw a monkey wrench into the wobbly relationship between the guy's mom and his girlfriend. Their unavoidable interference can serve, at the very least, as a distraction and, at worst, as an impairment.

The connection most likely to undermine the relationship between the boy's mom and his significant other is usually the one between the couple's two mothers (throw in any stepmoms and you essentially have a free-for-all). Whichever one has the ear of her child can easily create an imbalance in the couple's relationship.

Another person to likely upset the delicate rapport between the women is the son's father. Men love to emotionally high-five their sons. You know, like when they were little and they scored a goal? Now they high-five them for a different sort of score. And because a mother would never do this, she's automatically placed at a disadvantage.

Sometimes a grandparent or an aunt or a brother can comment adversely on a couple's relationship, resulting in a sustained chipping away of the developing bond between the women. We often can't do much to change the attitude of these intruding relatives, so it's best to just ignore them.

There is no mother like your own mother.
—Bambara proverb

My Mother/My Self

Angry over several incidents including a refusal to pay for her wedding, Emily hasn't spoken to her mother in two years. The beneficiary of this dysfunctional relationship is her mother-in-law, who has taken on the role of her mother.

Based on my interviews, there is a direct correlation between how a woman gets along with her own mother and how she gets along with her boyfriend's mom. A really close relationship between daughter and mother often results in a mother-in-law feeling like a third wheel or, worse yet, a pariah. A poor relationship between a daughter and mother, as in Emily's case, often makes room for a unique bond between the young woman and her mother-in-law.

Regardless of how a young woman feels toward each mother, she does have the power to make each one feel wanted, loved, and an integral part of the life she shares with their son or son-in-law.

Nonnie prefers being with her boyfriend's mom. "I love her. She's really awesome, and we're extremely close. My own mother is crazy, emotional, and dramatic, and I don't find it easy to talk to her. I don't hate her. I still speak with her. I'd just rather spend time with my boyfriend's mom."

This conflict between a daughter and her mother is rooted in a dynamic that transcends and predates the life she has with her boyfriend, and also with his mother. A mother-in-law is rarely the cause of this conflict, but she can, either wittingly or not, exacerbate it by the way she connects with the girlfriend. Nonnie admits that her mother is probably jealous of her relationship with her boyfriend's mom. "But I think she can make an effort to have some of the traits that his mother has. Things that make it so easy to spend time with her. She's more positive, has no judgments. My mother has certain expectations."

That's because she's her mom. By contrast, her mother-in-law appears to be less judgmental and critical. It's not that mothers-in-law don't judge, it's just that mothers of sons are going to do their best to stifle their true feelings in order to keep you, which means their son, in their lives. A guy's mother has little to gain and so much to lose if she's as honest with her daughter-in-law as she is with her own daughter.

Nonnie is angry with her mother for making her feel guilty for choosing to attend a holiday party with her boyfriend's family rather than go visit her cousin who had just adopted a baby. "My mom said this is a great time for your boyfriend to meet the rest of the family. But I had plans with my boyfriend's family. She made me feel terrible." To Nonnie's mother, her cousin's celebration took precedence over her boyfriend's party. The boyfriend's mom understood this, too. She told Nonnie that she imagined her mother must be upset over the amount of time she spends with their family. Nonnie, according to the boy's mother, "is bonded to her mom the same way I'm bonded to my daughters." In other words, Nonnie's mother-in-law would never tolerate her own daughters' disregard.

Whatever the reasons are for why these daughters are upset with their mothers, it is unlikely their mother wants to be dismissed for another woman. I wonder how many times getting close to a mother-in-law, whether calculated or not, is intended to punish the mother.

Janet's admission that she prefers her mother-in-law over her own mother isn't lost on her mom. "My mom says, 'You like your mother-in-law because she buys you things.' I say, 'You don't get it. It's because my mother-in-law makes me feel good about myself.' My mom doesn't. She's inconsiderate and inappropriate. I've always liked my mother-in-law. She's the type of mother my own mother is not."

In contrast, closeness between a woman and her mother can sometimes create distance between the woman and her mother-in-law. Marie was so close to her mother, who died before the birth of her first grandchild, that in comparison she finds her husband's mom to be annoying and thoughtless. "Not having my own mom magnifies the situation," Marie says. "I think my mom would have gotten involved and would have told off my mother-in-law. She would have amped it up. It would have been *my daughter versus your son*. So to some degree, it's a blessing she's not here. Early on in my relationship with my husband, my mother told me not to trust his mom. 'She's not your friend,' she warned me." Years later, those words still echo in Marie's head, and her relationship with her mother-in-law continues to deteriorate.

Like Marie, Jenny knows that her boyfriend's mom can never spoil the bond she has with her own mother. "I'm extremely close to my own mom, who is very different from his. My family is very welcoming, almost too embracing. In the beginning, my boyfriend found it to be intimidating and a little suffocating. We were operating under different paradigms. But now he feels comfortable with my family. This is why my relationship with his mother is so stark in contrast. Since my family accepts him, they don't think they are losing me to his family. But I'm sure there is a sense of loss to his mother." There is, and it's compounded by the closeness between Jenny and her mother. Even a kindhearted, affable mother-in-law can't help but feel excluded when the other two females are so close.

As the young man's wife or girlfriend, you could help the situation by recognizing his mother's insecurity and by making a sincere attempt to include her in your life. In the end, everyone benefits; your mother maintains her relationship with you, your boyfriend is unburdened, and his mother is, if not happy, then happier.

By the way, it is possible for a young woman to get along

equally well with her mother and her mother-in-law. It may take a perfect alignment of the stars—or at least three really considerate females. Because, as any woman who survived adolescent pajama parties knows, "two's company, three's a crowd."

Robert thinks his fiancée is extremely close to her mother, but he sees that she is trying to befriend his. "I definitely know that she can never feel as close to my mom as she is to her mom. I also know that she feels incredibly lucky to have my mom as her mother-in-law. She tries to please my mom. I see her going out of her way to make my mom happy. She'll often go talk to her, just the two of them. She wants to keep my mom in good spirits."

Melissa says despite having a very close relationship with her own mom, she considers her mother-in-law to be "mother-like. I am extremely close to my own mother, who's my best friend." She admits that her mother-in-law will never compare to her own mother because "that's a bond that is unlike any other. She does come second."

Mechutonim: Your Parental Counterpart

As the mother of a son who would rather talk animatedly to a television screen than to a human being, I always know the impact the other mother has on her daughter, and therefore on my son. A daughter, being female, is more likely to reveal details to her mom about her love life than a son is. That gives her parents an unfair advantage over the boy's parents—or as they say in Yiddish, the *mechutonim*. It's a little like when the New England Patriots got caught (sorry, I'm a Philadelphia Eagles fan) filming the opposing teams and went on to win the Super Bowl. It's impossible to compete with someone who has knowledge you don't.

It also sends these two mothers onto an unleveled playing

field. So what can the mother of the son do to communicate with the other mother? First of all, don't try to become best friends. Over the upcoming years a lot of events will change your feelings about each other; not the least of these will occur over wedding planning and grandchild raising. The best relationship between the *mechutonim* is one based on mutual respect, a recognition of inherent differences, and an appreciation for the children leading their own lives.

Neither mother should invest in a relationship with the other until the two kids have committed to each other, most likely with marriage or cohabitation. At that point, the two mothers who may have not gotten along before the wedding now must work at improving their relationship.

But what can a mother-in-law do if the daughter *wants* her mother involved in everything? As we discussed earlier, a girl can remain close to her mom, but once she's in a committed relationship she has to accept new boundaries. If she complains about her husband to her mom, her mother's opinion of him will be altered even if the couple resolves their issues.

If you, as the mother-in-law, think this other mother doesn't like your son, or if you think she intrudes too much in his life with her daughter, or if you just have nothing in common, you may find it impossible to like her. Rise above this, focusing instead on your relationship with her daughter. Not only will her daughter start to trust you, but when she's angry at her mother she'll turn to you.

Sue knows that she has been able to remain close to her daughter-in-law because the mom lives far away. Recently, though, the mother decided to move near her daughter, and Sue fears this may change the dynamics. "I liked it better when she was out of town," she admits. I understand how Sue feels. When the time comes, I would hate for my son to move close to his wife's mother and for me to feel completely out of the loop.

I can only hope that a mother of a daughter can appreciate the loss the mother of a son might feel. And I hope I can practice what I preach when my own daughter gets married.

Sometimes the girl's mother is just so unappealing or pushy that it's impossible for a guy's own mother to like her. Lily and her son's future mother-in-law are courteous when they see each other, but there is an undercurrent of bête noir that escapes neither of them. Lily says, "I was raised to get along with everybody and that was my job. I couldn't find a lot in common to share with her. I make an enormous effort. I give her a big hug, but she will never be a good friend."

Compounding Lily's dislike for the other mom is the knowledge that she constantly injects her opinion into the relationship between her daughter and Lily's son. "There is a closeness between mother and daughter that sometimes makes it feel as if there are three people in my son's relationship," adds Lily. "I wonder how much in their relationship has been influenced by the mom. I have more problems with her mother than with the girl."

As much as I advise mothers (and that includes me) to let the kids embrace their own relationship—with its pitfalls and rewards—sometimes the daughter chooses to invite her mom in. There's little the boy's mom can do about this other than maintain a caring, deferential relationship with both her son and his wife or girlfriend. There will be moments when it works to her benefit. For example, if the girl's mother remains overly involved in their lives, opining on every decision they should make as a couple from purchasing rugs to choosing preschools, it is only a matter of time before the guy seeks out a trusting sounding board: his mom.

Kelly knows her mother and boyfriend's mom don't get along, mainly because his mother remains in denial of the seriousness of her son's relationship. When she called Kelly's mom to tell her her son would reject her daughter after the prom, Kelly's mom responded sarcastically, "Your son knew my daughter since the fall dance and liked her and asked her to the prom. So don't get worried." The son's mom immediately backed down.

Caroline has learned how to get along with her daughter-in-law's mother by helping her see she isn't trying to push her out of her role as mother. "At first she was scared that I was going to steal her daughter because I got along so well with her, as did she. I think that changed slowly over the years because I was always nice to her and she saw all the things I did for her daughter. She became appreciative."

A mother of a daughter, no matter how close they are, will eventually welcome, even like, the guy's mother if she feels unthreatened, and if she thinks the other woman genuinely cares about her daughter. But sometimes the son's mom may actually have to remind the other mother that she has no intention of coming between her and her daughter. Caroline understands this, too. As close as she is to her daughter-in-law, she has told her mother, "You are her only mother. I am here as a pinch hitter when you can't get to her."

Nicely put.

The Son and Her Family

In the first years of my marriage to Charlie, my parents were polite but not yet fully accepting of this man whose background appeared to be so different from their daughter's. So Charlie and I spent most of our time with his family. His parents embraced me unconditionally, and I looked forward to going to his home for the Christmas holidays, relishing the smells of his mom's baking and the sights of her festive living room—charmingly overadorned with plastic Santas, revolving trees, and cutesy stockings. It was with a certain amount of dread that we would venture to my disenchanted family for the holidays.

But that feeling improved, and in fact vanished, as my parents allowed themselves to get to know my husband and discover all the reasons I loved him. Ten years later, when my father became ill, it was Charlie with whom he wanted to spend time.

We, and by that I mean our two mothers as well, were fortunate that Charlie and I both wanted a relationship with each other's parents and recognized the importance of keeping our families in our lives. If I had limited the time with his family and insisted we spend more time with mine, his relationship with his parents would have suffered. Since we were of different religions, we celebrated many holidays together with our respective families, and on broader occasions, such as Thanksgiving and Mother's Day, I invited both families to my home. Now that I have a son who dates, I realize how grateful my mother-in-law must have felt that her daughter-in-law never excluded her.

Ever since Paul got married, he has grown close to his wife's family and a little more distant from his own. Simultaneously, his mother has become friendlier to her other daughter-in-law, the wife of Paul's brother, who has a poor relationship with her own mother. This devotion to their respective in-laws has created a little tension between Paul and his mom.

"I spend less time with my mom, but our love for each other hasn't changed," he says. "That's the sacrifice I'm willing to make for my brother and his wife. They need her more," he adds as justification. "I haven't been jealous that my mom spends more time and is closer with my sister-in-law than with my wife. I understand but it changes the dynamics."

The consequences of a guy getting close to his girlfriend's family usually means less time with his own. Most men (my apologies to those who aren't this way) find it easier to tag along with their wives and not create disagreement by insisting on equal time with their family. That's good for the girl's family, but bad for his. Paul admits that his mother-in-law is "like another mom to me. But my relationship with my own mom has definitely changed. We don't talk on the phone or see each other as much. I know that we still love each other very much so I'm okay with it."

But is she? Mothers of sons prepare themselves to let go— not without pain—but mothers of daughters don't. It's no surprise that a son's relationship with his wife's family will be affected by how she gets along with them. If she's close to her parents, as is Paul's wife, then he probably will be. If she's not, like Paul's sister-in-law, then he won't be.

As Lily says, "It's a powerful influence—the relationship between the girl [and] a parent." And that influence will ultimately power the union between the man and his significant other.

When my son dated the young woman with the improperly proper mother, I had no idea what he thought of her parents. If I commented on the mother being a little too involved in, say, my son and his girlfriend's plans for the summer, he remained silent, expressionless. I really didn't know what he was thinking. But when the relationship ended, he admitted to me: "I didn't like her mother. I liked her dad. I also never said a thing to my girlfriend about what I thought of her mother. But I do think she [his girlfriend] honestly liked you." And why not? I'm the mother of the boy; I know when to keep mum.

Distance has prevented Rebecca from getting to know her son's girlfriend. Yet the girl's parents live near the young couple and, consequently, have gotten to know her son very well. "He's with her family all the time. I'm happy with that. I want him to get along with them."

Lily says the parents of her son's girlfriend thinks he "walks on water." And her daughter—his younger sister—adds that that makes her family feel like the "unwelcoming ones." In actuality, as soon as this girlfriend starts to feel more welcomed by her boyfriend's family, he'll bring her around more. If she doesn't, it will, as with Paul, just be easier for the son to visit her parents who welcome him with open arms.

Counselor Ganz says, "Girls and guys don't just get together with each other, they get together with each other's family. Sometimes they seek out what they missed in their own lives and get very attached [like Janet and Nonnie]. You may be dealing with a woman feeling abandoned by her mother, emotionally and not necessarily physically."

That's the case with Cindy. Her daughter-in-law became close to her because she wasn't getting the love and attention she needed from her own parents. Her father, in addition, treated Cindy's son so horribly that the two men stopped communicating. "When he first made my son's life miserable, his girlfriend told me, 'That's how my father always treats the boys I date.' I told her, 'You're not dating a boy anymore, you're dating a man.' My son wasn't going to take crap from her parents, and after they got married, it got worse and worse. In the end my daughter-in-law chose my son over her parents. I felt, on one hand, I can't understand how you can give up on your parents, but seeing how they treat my son, I can understand."

All relationships are based on compromise. If a woman is close to her parents and her boyfriend or husband is close to his, they should both make every effort to include each other's families. If a man's mother feels left out, then she has to make the overtures: invite the couple over, or meet the younger woman's family at a restaurant to celebrate her son's new job or her daughter-in-law's promotion. She should find reasons to get together, and not stand on ceremony waiting for an invitation from them. It may not come, and the distance between her and her son will grow.

If the younger woman feels she's being excluded from her boyfriend's family, then she needs to tell him, and he needs to inform his family that when he comes, she comes, too.

The father is always a Republican toward his son, and his mother's always a Democrat.
—Robert Frost

Father (Thinks He) Knows Best

Betty dropped off laundry in her son's room, and noticed a note "bold as day" lying on the floor. It was from a girl in his twelfth-grade class. "It was terribly suggestive with comments like 'I can't wait to sit on you and feel you.' I was outraged, disgusted. I never told my son that I had found it, but I told my husband."

And his reaction? No outrage. No disgust. Just "All right, Matt!"

This is a fairly typical reaction of one male's learning that another male has reached a certain level of, well, maleness, and helps explain why the boy's father is often more accepting of the young woman.

"The things that were important to me are different from his father," Betty says. "Maybe the girl will connect with me, raise their children well, be classy and smart and a full partner. And can take care of him. I'm thinking all of this, and my husband is thinking, *Matt's happy, and she's pretty.*"

Parenthetically, men don't get off that easy when the romance they are reacting to involves their daughter, rather than their son. In that case, they act a lot like the mother. According to Dr. Lazaroff, "Fathers are a lot more crazed because they think they're losing their little princess." While sons relinquish the role of Mamma's Boy as they age, daughters never stop being Daddy's Little Girl.

Even if mothers understand this difference in perspectives between themselves and their husbands, it can be infuriating when they're trying to establish a good relationship with their son's significant other. If she isn't caring and attentive, they couldn't care less about her looks.

Jill's ex-husband, with whom she's maintained a genuinely loving relationship, thinks their son's girlfriend, whom Jill describes as "nasty," is just great, and good-looking. Needless to say, the girl likes the dad. This discrepancy in opinion is not uncommon if the guy's parents are divorced. The presence of this girlfriend is much less threatening to the dad than to the mom because it lacks the competition of same-gender relationships. Also, the relationship between the father and son won't necessarily change with the introduction of a woman. Accept the fact that you, as a mom, will never compete with the father's easygoing relationship with your son's significant other. So don't even try. Be the mother in the relationship—which, if you're lucky, might even translate into being a girlfriend to the girlfriend.

In the case of a contentious divorce, you may be frustrated to find that your son and his girlfriend would rather be with your ex-husband, who's not observing, judging, or assessing their relationship. He's not even really noticing it. You, on the other hand, pick up on everything. And the girlfriend, also being female, knows you do. Some girlfriends may take advantage of this discord between the guy's parents, purposely getting close with one and not the other.

Marie admits that she spends more time with her husband's stepfather than his mother, and that really infuriates the mom. The mom is divorced from both her son's biological father, whom he doesn't see, and his stepfather. She knows how close her son and his wife are with the stepdad and children from another marriage and often calls her son at work to complain. "I don't know what kind of ideas your wife is putting in your head or why you are friends with Bob [the stepdad who raised him]. But how do you think that makes me feel?" his mother whines.

"I have to keep them separated," Marie says. "For my husband's birthday we had to plan it around the two parents. His mother would be with the stepdad, but he doesn't want to be with her. So we planned for dinner Friday night with the dad, and Sunday brunch with the mom." Unaware the mother was at the house, the stepdad stopped by with presents. "We cracked up. Here we tried for three weeks choreographing this so you wouldn't see each other and here you are."

Marie's mother-in-law deals with her own insecurities; not being in a relationship herself and having her ex-husband re-married. Her son can't help her solve these issues, but he could improve her relationship with him, which in turn would improve her relationship with Marie; subsequently, any closeness to his dad would matter less.

Twenty-eight-year-old Joe, whose parents are divorced, acknowledges that he's much closer to his dad than to his mom. When he was fifteen and his parents separated, he first moved in with his mother. Admittedly, Joe's primary disciplinarian and caretaker through high school was his mother, so it has been easier to have a "friendship" with his dad. His father likes Joe's girlfriend. "They get along well," Joe says. "Whenever he wants to get together for dinner, he always invites her along. When she's not there, he asks about her."

Joe's mom, on the other hand, has been less accepting of his girlfriend. She's losing her son to another woman, and that other woman is friends with the man she divorced. To compensate, Joe's mother has been trying to befriend his girlfriend, if only to confide in her about her divorce, telling her details her son never mentioned and effectively turning her against the dad. "It's hard to look at his father now," Joe's girlfriend says. "I look at him differently because he married the woman with whom he cheated on his mom. The conversation has been something of a bonding experience for me and his mom."

Both Marie's husband and Joe need to speak one-on-one with their mothers and explain that their significant others would like to have a relationship with both the father and the mother. One doesn't need to preclude the other. And if the moms can't open up to this, they may find themselves estranged from their sons, which is something no one wants.

In some divorces, the father may not be all that interested in the son's love life, and the wife or girlfriend will almost certainly feel closer to his mom. Hope says that although her son called her first to tell her he was engaged, she wasn't surprised because she knew they were serious. Her ex-husband, on the other hand, had no inkling and was shocked. Their son and daughter-in-law, according to Hope, do not like the dad's new wife, which consequently improves Hope's relationship with them.

A son's parents don't have to be divorced for there to be a different relationship between each of them and the wife or girlfriend. William says his mother gets along with his girlfriend, but his father is uninvolved. "I don't know if he knows I have a girlfriend," he says, sarcastically. William's girlfriend says after six years of dating, his father incredibly still introduces himself to her by his first and last name.

The Extended Family

Sometimes other members of the family will try to evaluate a couple's relationship, and if they have enough clout to influence it, they can serve as an added benefit or diversion. My grandparents and my sister accepted Charlie long before my parents did, but that had no bearing on my relationship with him. It did, however, make me feel better.

That's not the situation in Joe's case. Quiet and reserved, he doesn't fit into his girlfriend's huge and boisterous clan. Although he gets along with her three sisters, her dad, and for the most part her mom, the mom's sister is "always taking shots at me."

Invariably, he dreads the visits with her lively family where everyone talks at once. "I'm the quiet one and don't try to get involved in shouting matches, and they take that as my not being interested or not being engaged." When a gathering is over, and everyone kisses and hugs, Joe shouts out an all-encompassing "See you later, everybody." His girlfriend's aunt angrily tells her sister that Joe's rude. "I don't think my girl-friend's mom would ever take my side over the aunt's. I'm get-ting tired of hearing the same thing over and over again. 'He's quiet. He didn't say good-bye to everybody.' They've known me for eight years. It's not going to change."

At one family party, Joe tried to say good-bye to everyone in-dividually, but when he reached the aunt, she was engaged in a particularly animated conversation so he skipped over her rather than interrupt. Someone in the room egged her on. "Aunt Karen, did Joe say good-bye?" She said, "No!" And Joe just turned around and walked out the door. "I can't win," he says.

We all have at least one family member who in some way tries to influence the relationship between the couple. This in-trusion can cause a little friction between the son and his wife or girlfriend, or between one of them and the other's parents. It may be an extended family member or it can be another sibling, as discussed in the previous chapter.

Nonnie finds that her older sister's opinions impact her par-ents' perspective on her relationship with her boyfriend. "My sister is on a pedestal," Nonnie says, "and my parents accept her advice as gospel. I've come to realize that she doesn't know everything. I understand it's been difficult for my parents be-cause I've changed and my sister hasn't, but she can be chal-lenging for my relationship with my boyfriend."

Marie's sisters comment on her relationship, too, but as with Joe, it's because her family is large and her sisters are very close. "I talk to them every day and we have a set of cousins we're close with." After all this time, she says her husband has finally "grown to appreciate that, and my sisters have grown to love my husband."

Mother-in-Law's Mother-in-Law

The mothers-in-law who are accepting of their son's spouse often had their own mother-in-law as a role model. But many of the mothers I interviewed who consider themselves to be in great relationships with their son's wife or girlfriend had a lousy relationship with their husband's mom. It's Confucius's spin on the Golden Rule: "Never impose on others what you would not choose for yourself."

To a lot of these mothers, it's too late to reverse the contention they experienced with their mothers-in-law, but they now understand how those women must have felt, and they don't want to feel that way with their own daughters-in-law. Instead, they go out of their way to be nice.

Nicci, who raves about her son's serious girlfriend, admits that she didn't have a good relationship with her own mother-in-law. "She was very formal and proper and I found her to be really annoying and not a fun person. Plus, I just wanted to be close to my own mom and didn't want to let this other woman into my life. I was not a wonderful daughter-in-law. I blame myself. She would have liked to have been closer, but it was me."

As with so many daughters, Nicci encouraged her husband to become friendly to her family, at the loss of his own. "He was a dutiful son. Maybe he'd do an errand, visit his mother every week, but I never went. If I could go back and do it over again, I would be a better daughter-in-law. It would have been a better role model for my kids."

She could never accept her son's girlfriend treating her the same way she treated her mother-in-law. "I would kill myself if she ever viewed me the way I viewed my mother-in-law. That's why I work really hard at being close, but at the same time keeping my distance, and never being judgmental."

For many women who, once they become mothers-in-law themselves, realize they hadn't been a very kind daughter-in-law, it's too late to change the past. Fortunately for Amy, she's had time to renew a relationship with her in-laws following a decade of no communication. They stopped talking initially after Amy's husband told his parents that he and his wife were having marital problems and she wanted to leave the marriage. "It didn't matter what the problems were," Amy explains. "It only mattered that my mother-in-law's son wasn't happy, and it had to be my fault. I was the bitch."

The family reunited when Amy's son got married. After the invitations went out, she received an email from her sister-in-law requesting they get together to talk. "I said I'd talk to her but she'd have to listen to what I had to say, too. I had ten years to think about this. Now it's fine. His sister is a warm and loving person. My son's wedding brought everything to a head."

Drawing from these experiences, Amy says she now has good advice for her own son if he should ever tell her he's unhappy in his marriage. "I hope I would have the foresight to say, 'You have a lot of years. You have kids. Maybe she did this, and maybe it's because you did that.' I hope I would be open enough to say that and give him what I didn't get from my in-laws, which is support."

Cindy blames her mother-in-law for their poor relationship, and so she tries to get along with her own daughter-in-law. "I was young and naïve when I got married and I came from a close-knit family. I assumed I would be part of that again. I assumed that she'd be another mom to me, and I'd be the daughter she never had. In her defense, she never said she wanted a daughter. I was shocked by her coldness. I attributed a lot of her reserve to the fact that she was European, a different cultural upbringing. She was cold emotionally, not just to me, but to my husband." In contrast, Cindy exudes warmth and love for her daughter-in-law, with whom she has developed a very close relationship.

Both Meg and Hope had mothers-in-law whom—no matter

how hard they tried—they could never please, and both act, while not overbearingly nurturing, respectful and noninterfering with their own daughters-in-law. "I didn't get along with my mother-in-law," Hope says. "She didn't like me. She was sweet, sweet, sweet, and then mean. The sun rose and set on her son, and I don't know what she wanted, but it wasn't me." Today, Hope says, she treats her own son and his wife with love and never voices an opinion about their marriage.

Of course, not all women need to have had a bad relationship with their mother-in-law to learn a lesson and be kind to their son's significant other. Linda says she loved her mother-in-law. "If I asked her opinion, she wouldn't give it to me. I don't go that far! My mother-in-law once told me I could come live with her, but her son couldn't."

Sibling-in-Law Rivalry

A significant force in family dynamics is the relationship between the two daughters-in-law, the wives of the brothers. Especially if these women represent the only "daughters" in a woman's life, they can find themselves in direct competition for their mother-in-law's attention.

Paul's fiancée couldn't wait to ask his brother's wife if she would be a bridesmaid. They thought she'd appreciate the honor and wouldn't hesitate to reply with an enthusiastic "Yes!" Instead she told them she would have to think about it. "It was like a slap in the face," says Paul. "My fiancée was shocked and upset. But my sister-in-law is a very different type of person. My fiancée and I are empathy freaks. But when it comes to empathy, my sister-in-law is pretty under the radar. It's not even there."

Paul's brother had gotten married a few years before him, and his wife enjoyed being the only *daughter* in the family. Then Paul became engaged. His mother also noticed the tension. She says, "She had been daughter number one. Then along comes daughter number two. The first one wasn't nice, and the other one is sensitive..We didn't want them coming between the boys. My husband and I would say we were a close-knit family before the girls came along."

Paul says when his mother, who is closer to his brother's wife than to his, once went for a walk with his fiancée, his sister-in-law became upset. "You could see her shoulders stiffen a bit. 'Why didn't they wait for me?'"

The trouble here is that while a mother can tell a daughter to get over it and stop acting so peevishly, she frets about being so honest with her son's wife. But she knows if the two women don't get along, then future family get-togethers will be contentious or, worse, nonexistent.

Dr. Lazaroff acknowledges that these situations in which the two daughters-in-law don't get along can be tricky. "On the one hand, direct communication is always best," she says. "On the other hand, the mother-in-law is an in-law herself and probably does not want to offend either daughter-in-law for fear of losing good relations with her sons and grandchildren."

She suggests that the mother speak to her sons, telling them that for the sake of their family it would be helpful if they could try to understand the nature of the conflict, and then encourage the two wives to speak to each other to resolve it. "This way," Lazaroff adds, "the mother-in-law does not offend the women but may be able to resolve the difficulties between them. If the air can't be cleared between the two daughters-in-law, then the husbands need to tell them that they at least have to be decent and civil to each other at family gatherings."

The additional problem she sees is that with a domineering wife, the husband may not always have the strength to speak up. As a result, he'll either see his family on his own time or risk losing them.

Ganz says that if this should be the case, then the mother-in-law should meet with the women individually and ask them to help problem solve or negotiate a compromise. "I think sons could be in denial of possible consequences of their wives not getting along," she says. Although a mother-in-law may worry about having this one-on-one conversation with each daughter-in-law, she may be surprised at their reactions. Rather than making her the heavy, they will each try to curry her favor.

Some mothers-in-law actually help create a tension between their sons' significant others by overtly showing favor toward one. In this situation, she should consider her sons' best interests, and stop facilitating a sibling rivalry between their spouses. Kelly's boyfriend's mom is purposely doing this. "His mom is always nicer to the girlfriend of my boyfriend's brother than to me. She's just so happy that his brother has somebody that she's not going to do anything to jeopardize it. It makes me jealous a little bit."

She says her boyfriend is not responsive when she complains about this. "He thinks I'm crazy. But they hang out and go to dinner, and I keep thinking back to the time I asked her to go to dinner and she turned me down."

Although there is often conflict between the wives of the sons, sometimes, especially if there are any sisters in the family, the wives actually get very close. It's really out of necessity, a kind of divide and conquer. If they feel like outsiders in their husbands' family, they will be naturally drawn to the other wives. In Joan's family, for example, she says that the wives of her two brothers have gotten very close and don't bother competing for the attention of Joan and her sisters. "They are both quiet and reserved, so at family gatherings I do see them bonding."

Let's face it, we can try our best to get along with a son's wife, or a husband's mother and sister, but we have only limited control in how the nonblood relatives get along. Linda knows she is fortunate that there is genuine fondness among her three son's wives, all of whom have no sisters themselves. "When your in-law children like one another, that is something you can't plan," Linda says. "It's a truly wonderful feeling."

———

Dealing with mandatory issues such as finances, child rearing, and living arrangements can put stress on any couple—even those who've worked hard to find compromise and mutual appreciation. Such a couple benefit from the support of as many family members as possible and need not be sidetracked by those who would refuse to give it. Their relationship is really about two people—each other.

Keepsakes

1. The guy's significant other has some clout in making each mom—hers and his—feel a part of their life.

2. A mom should be cordial to the other mom, but the two don't need to be best friends.

3. If a guy gets closer to his girlfriend's family, he naturally pulls away from his own. He and his girlfriend should recognize this and make every effort to be inclusive.

4. Throw a divorced parent into the mix and the possibility of hurt feelings increases. Everyone needs to be more empathetic.

5. All those extraneous people—sisters-in-law, ex-spouses, grandparents, and others—should focus on their own relationships.

CHAPTER SEVEN

Sex, Marriage, and Cohabitation

Lydia tossed a couple of frozen waffles into the toaster, washed and cut up strawberries, and flipped on the coffeemaker. On this particular morning she thought she'd surprise her seventeen-year-old son by topping his waffles with a dollop of whipped cream. She had no idea he had a surprise for her, too.

He ambled into the kitchen still bleary-eyed from sleep and wearing the boxers and faded T-shirt that served as pajamas. Behind him, walked a teenage girl, mindlessly twisting her silky hair with her fingers.

"Mom, this is Patty. Patty, Mom," said her son, never short on manners.

Lydia, too stunned to question or to chastise, merely sputtered "Uh, do you want a waffle, too?"

"Sure," chirped Patty, unfazed about having spent the night. "But skip the whipped cream."

Although the warning signs are always there—his voice gravitates downward, his stance expands upward, his feet grow out-ward, and his language shrinks—no mother actually antici-pates the moment when she learns her son is sexually active. She has spent his entire childhood preparing him for the fu-ture, encouraging him to study so he can find a good job or get into a top college, pushing him to excel at sports or art or music to ease his entry into cutthroat adolescence, and insist-ing he maintain his appearance by wearing clean clothes, tak-ing showers, and combing his hair. And when, just shy of puberty, she or his father has the "sex talk" with him, she ex-pects him to absorb, then table, that information.

Mothers know that once he adds sex to his list of firsts, like his first shave or his first car, he enters an adult world through a door that locks behind him. Ahead of him are love, commit-ment, cohabitation, marriage, and more sex. If moms thought potty training and passing algebra were their greatest chal-lenges in raising a son, then, as songwriter Randy Bachman wrote in the 1970s, "You Ain't Seen Nothing Yet."

For the girlfriends of these sons, once your relationship in-cludes sex, it's a little discomfiting to act as though you're celi-bate in front of his mother. You stayed in his dorm room all semester, and as far as you're concerned you don't want to be shuttled to the guest room when you visit his family. His mom, though, has already put fresh linens on the bed.

And sex is just the beginning. If you and your boyfriend de-cide to marry, you will now find yourself saddled with not only your mother, but his mother as well. You want a small, private wedding in the backyard, while his mother wants to invite all her book club friends and is offering to pay for them, too.

If the girlfriend and the boy's mother can weather the wed-ding planning and still like each other the morning after, their future relationship may indeed be strong.

Getting an early start on the champagne couldn't hurt, either.

The trouble with boys is that they must become men.
—Angela Marie Phillips, feminist and journalist

Let's Talk About Sex

Everyone remembers the first time she had sex. If you're the mother of a son, you also remember the first time you realized your son did.

You may have found a crumbled note tossed under his bed (you looked, we all do). Or discovered a condom packet on the floor of your car (no wonder he had uncharacteristically offered to wash it). Or inadvertently overheard a conversation or read a text message never intended for your perusal. It's a memorable moment—one met with a mixture of awe, discomfort, and a little denial.

Different mothers react differently to this development. Some ignore the discovery and silently pray that the safe-sex conversation they had years before has found its way into his stream of consciousness. Others leave nothing to chance, driving to the nearest drugstore to buy their sons condoms. Those mothers, incidentally, are not necessarily sanctioning or encouraging their sons to have sex. They accept the situation as being completely out of their control and want their sons to be as safe as possible. It's the same justifiable hypocrisy that occurs when a parent counsels her minor-age child not to drink, then when he starts to drive, offers to pick him up—no questions asked—if he ever finds himself drinking.

A boy's mother may find that while she doesn't approve of a young couple having sex, the girlfriend's parents might, especially if they like her son. If this is the case (mothers of daughters probably had the birth control conversation at some point around the onset of menstruation), a son isn't going to listen to his mother if she disapproves. Fortunately, more often than not the girl's parents are just as against her having sex as you are for your son.

Jill says she wasn't startled so much to discover that her son was sexually active as that the girl's mother was compliant. "The mom called me and told me her daughter was on the pill and they accepted the fact that she was having sex with my son. I said I didn't want to discuss this with her. I told her, 'My son's sex life is none of my business.' She said it was okay with them because she and her husband liked my son."

Knowing full well that she would have little power to stop the intimacy between her son and his girlfriend, Jill decided to lecture her son on the importance of using condoms, and mailed some to his dorm. Betty also was surprised that the parents of her son's girlfriend had given their daughter permission to have sex. "I would have thought that the parents would have been more worried and strict. Instead they were all in this and didn't set any limits."

Because a boy's mom has no idea whether the girl has taken precautions, the responsibility to make sure the guy is aware of safe-sex issues can fall to his mother. Kids obtain a lot of information, and misinformation, from television, movies, and their friends. Even if your son has sex education in school, it's important that by the time he enters puberty, you or someone close to him has reinforced in him safe-sex practices.

When he actually starts to engage in sex, the conversation becomes less of a how-to guide than a very personalized discussion about the risks involved and ways to avoid them. A mom should be able to get past any feeling of awkwardness in order to have this conversation with her son. He needs to be told (again) that even if the female he is sleeping with or is thinking about sleeping with takes birth control pills, that doesn't protect against sexually transmitted diseases such as HIV. A condom will.

Hope says she spoke to her son when he was in high school, using basketball star Magic Johnson, who tested positive for HIV, as an example. "I remember telling my son don't ever believe a woman if she says she can't get pregnant. When he went away to college, I bought him condoms."

When a son discovers sex, passion will confuse his intelligence and reasonability. He will benefit from a talk with his mom or his dad. Even though there's no guarantee he will follow through, there is no doubt he will have heard them.

Sleepovers

Back in the late 1960s, when Josie and Jack started dating, most parents expected their children to abstain from sex until after they were married. So when Josie, just nineteen, joined her boyfriend and his family on a vacation, the men stayed in one room, the women in another. A short time after everyone went to sleep, there was a knock on the women's door. "Jack was standing there with a pillow," Josie reminisces. "He said he couldn't stay in the other room because they snored. His mother said, 'You can't stay here; Josie's here.' She let him in, but she slept in the bed between us. We spent our entire trip like that."

It's unlikely today that a mother of a son would choose to reenact this role of human contraceptive, but that doesn't mean she's ambivalent about the goings-on in her own home. Despite her knowledge that most college students live in coed dorms, and that work colleagues often share a hotel suite or an apartment when they travel for their job, she's uncomfortable allowing sexual intimacy between her son and a girlfriend under her roof.

The first time Noah brought a girlfriend home from college, he accepted my requirement that they sleep in separate rooms. Even though I knew they were probably staying together back at school, I was entitled to set some rules in my home. A couple of years later when he returned home with a different and serious girlfriend, who had practically lived in his dorm room the entire semester, I presented the same set of rules.

"Come on, Mom," he argued.

"Humor me" was my brilliant parenting advice.

"No. That's ridiculous," he countered, actually becoming upset.

"Then can you at least sleep in a sleeping bag on the floor of your room and give her your bed?" I can't believe I was relenting.

"Fine, Mom," he growled.

The conversation ended with both of us knowing that he'd unroll the sleeping bag on his floor but would sleep wherever he chose. But I, at least, had maintained a shred of self-respect.

Some girlfriends are unaware that this sort of conversation takes place. While some guys will relate the details, others don't want to admit that when they are back in their mother's home they are going to follow rules suitable for when they were younger. After all, now that he is sexually active, which translates in his mind to worldly and mature, he will do as he chooses. So he says to his girlfriend, "It's cool. You can stay in my room."

Or he says nothing and just acts as though their staying together is uneventful. Robert admits that once he entered college, he never asked his mother for permission to have a girlfriend stay over. Instead, he and the young woman headed downstairs to his basement bedroom. "Mom never said anything to me," he says. "I don't know if she knew because I don't recall our seeing my mom the next morning." Believe me, regardless of whether the mother and the young woman come face-to-face, the mother is well aware that someone is with her son behind his closed door. Otherwise she would have knocked.

So here is a word of advice to the girlfriend: Don't assume

that your boyfriend is telling you the truth when he says his mother approves. Whether the mother does, or doesn't, isn't the issue. It's that you show gratitude for being a guest in her home. Ask her, not him, where she would like you to sleep. If she directs you to a room other than her son's, honor her request even though it seems ridiculous for you to pretend you're not having sex with a guy you've been sleeping with for months. She will appreciate that you respected her wishes and that, regardless of what her son told you, you were more concerned about her feelings. It's not that his mother is asking or expecting you two to abstain; she just wants to maintain some control in her surroundings. If this relationship with this man has a future, you have endeared yourself to his mother.

Caroline says that when her son and his girlfriend were in high school, she sometimes would allow her to sleep over, but in separate rooms. The two willingly agreed to her rules. At any rate, that's what they told her. One morning they came into the kitchen unknowingly wearing each other's bottoms. "I looked at his girlfriend and said, 'You might want to go back and change.' She looked down and turned beet red. I told them, once again, I didn't want anything happening in my house."

If your son has only recently discovered girls or started dating, you're probably thinking you would never allow a girl to stay in his room. That's what all mothers think, at least at one time. But once a son graduates from high school or leaves home, it becomes much more difficult to exercise the same control. After all, you miss him, and if you can make his visit home wonderful, he'll come home again, and again. Preparing his favorite dinner of prime rib and twice-baked potatoes isn't enough of an enticement when he's older. Treating him as an adult when it involves his social life is. (Treating him like a little boy when it involves doing his laundry is, too.) Still, it's your home—the girl can come, but she should sleep where you want her to.

Betty says that when her son's girlfriend stayed over in high school, he gave her his bed and he slept on the sofa. Once they started college, he told his mom that he would sleep in a sleeping bag on the floor of his room and his girlfriend would take his bed. And, like most mothers, Betty fantasized that that's how it stayed. "I'm a realist," Betty says. "Even though it freaked me out a little bit, I knew they were sleeping together at school. I wanted them to feel normal and comfortable and welcomed in my home. Now they just go in and close the door."

Linda always used the possible corruption of her youngest son as an excuse not to allow her two older boys have girls stay in their rooms. "I'd tell them they had to sleep in separate rooms. But in the middle of the night I'd hear noises. When they woke up in the morning, though, they'd be back in separate rooms. By the time my youngest started dating, my defenses were down. He didn't even ask permission to have a girl stay over."

Many factors influence a mother's decision regarding sleepovers. As Dr. Lazaroff says, there can be religious, moral, or behavioral reasons for why an unmarried couple cannot sleep together in the parents' home. "They already know that this will never happen in our house," Lazaroff says. "When the girlfriend comes over she'll spend the night in the guest room." The concept is not up for debate.

"But in other cases," Lazaroff adds, "it may be a matter of negotiating with your son. He'll say, 'We stay together at school, so would you give us permission to stay together here, too?' He's already over eighteen and has been sexual with one woman and now another. You're not going to go back to kindergarten with this issue. When a precedent is set, it's hard to revisit it."

You're not getting the genie back in the bottle. So even though you think giving your son permission to have his long-term girlfriend stay over in his room is case-specific, don't think he does. When the two break up and he next brings home a girl he barely knows, even though you can see a difference between the two situations, he won't. Once a mother has permitted her son to have a girl stay over, she's cleared the way for all future guests.

Jenny's boyfriend's mother won't let that happen at her house. She made it clear years ago that no couple—unless they were married or engaged—could stay together in her home. "And," Jenny says, "this rule hasn't been breached since." So when she stays overnight, she is expected to sleep on the couch or in one of the sisters' rooms.

Lily appreciates that her son's girlfriend and her son, for that matter, have shown her the courtesy to not ask permission and to automatically choose separate rooms. "She doesn't spend the night that often but never are they both in the same room. I would feel uncomfortable facing his younger sisters. I consider myself liberal, but with this I would have a hard time."

And April wouldn't allow her son's girlfriend to spend the night until they were engaged. "My son had a close friend in high school. They were friends only. I said, 'Where is she going to stay?' and he said, 'In my room.' I said, 'Not in my house. That's disrespectful to her and to me.' Finally he gave in and slept on the sofa. I'm still living down that he considers me terribly old-fashioned."

Old-fashioned or not, April slept like a log.

Double Standards and Double Beds

As a mother, while you may be concerned about appearing too strict regarding sleepovers, be aware that the parents of your child's significant other have set their own set of standards—and they may, or may not, be similar to yours.

Twenty-two-year-old William says his girlfriend's parents have always allowed him to sleep in her room, though she has never been allowed to stay in his. "Her mom is totally cool and doesn't have a problem with it. I've slept at her house ten times as much as she has at mine. But I wouldn't feel comfortable asking my mom if she can stay in my room. What do I gain from going through that awkward conversation? The answer is going to be 'No. Not at my house,' anyway. I know my girlfriend gets on me about that sometimes. I keep finding a way to get out of it. I don't know if it's laziness on my part or wanting to avoid the awkwardness."

In Kelly's parents' home, her boyfriend is not welcomed to stay in her room, though she can stay overnight in his. "It just sort of happened. I fell asleep in there and when I left I said thank you to his mom for letting me stay over. It was weird in the beginning and I tried to leave before she got up. But now when I see her, I always thank her." This is basic good manners. If you are a guest in the home of your significant other, show appreciation to his mother—or her mother, for that fact—for allowing you to do so.

Paul says he never understood the double standard of his being allowed to stay at his girlfriend's home but her not being allowed to sleep at his. He had initially assumed it would be okay. It wasn't. "She stayed over once in high school and my mom let me have it. 'Don't you ever try that again.' I was thoroughly surprised because I had stayed over my girlfriend's house and it was not even questioned, and then she stayed at my house and it was like the world was going to stop spinning." No, it's not the end of the world, but families have different values. You—whether you are the man or the woman—have to respect those of your significant other in their family's presence.

Nicci not only allows her son's girlfriend to stay over—even though the invitation isn't reciprocated because of her family's religious beliefs—but also affords her two younger daughters the same privileges. "It's not an issue in our house," Nicci says.

"I don't think I would like it if every Friday night my daughters brought a different guy home, but I'm okay with their having a boyfriend stay."

Melissa says that before she and her husband became engaged, she'd sleep in his room, which had two bunk beds. But in her parents' home, the two always had to stay in separate rooms until they were married. "I was always surprised that his parents were okay with this because mine weren't," she says.

There are no set rules for who can sleep where and when. It's personal and based on each individual family's beliefs and wishes. In a situation in which a young couple want to sleep together in a parent's house, they must defer to the parent. Most parents with children older than high school age will accept at least the appearance of their sleeping apart and then will conveniently shut their own bedroom door at night.

It's like the Maurice Sendak book *Where the Wild Things Are*. Anything can happen once you're asleep.

The Announcement: Marriage or Moving In

Okay, Mom, this has all been part of your training for your eventual role as mother-in-law. Relationships with these girls you have (hopefully) so carefully tended to now are about to fully evolve—one way or another. But first: Consider how you handled having little to no influence in stopping your son from having sex as practice for your even lesser role now. If your son decides to live with or marry his girlfriend, it will be *their* decision.

You have the following choices:

Option One: You can disown him;

Option Two: You can suggest he rethink this positively terrible decision;

Option Three: You can express your support but gently recommend he consider certain issues, whether they be religious differences, money problems, or something else;

Option Four: You can open your arms, give him—and her— a hug and a kiss, and say, "I wish you both nothing but happiness."

If it's the first two options, you should expect to see a lot less of your son, and you need to decide if that is the outcome for which you're striving. If you select the third option—lending your support but with a realistic caveat—you may have planted a kernel of doubt by asking him to think a little deeper before making this hugely important decision. And (this is the critical part) regardless of his choice, he has your full support. If the marriage or cohabitation comes to an end, by using option three you've shut no doors. Your son will feel he can come to you to talk and you won't judge him. Keep in mind that you have only one opportunity to instill this thought process in him. If you do it repeatedly, you will effectively turn him away.

If you choose the last option, you've raised the possibility of having a loving relationship with not only your son, but also his significant other. Since planning a marriage or moving in together is always stressful, it won't take much—a misconstrued comment or an unanswered email—and you, as his mom, will take on the persona of the Wicked Witch. If you appreciate how taxing a time this is for them and offer them a safety net rather than let them free-fall, your relationships are bound to flourish.

Most mothers of sons will find it difficult, though necessary, to wait until they're asked to offer an opinion. If the couple chooses to get married on the busiest wedding day of the year or to paint their apartment chartreuse, recognize that they are the ones who have to live with their choice—not you. And before you voice any opinion, ask *her* what she prefers.

When my son and his girlfriend (I know I said I wouldn't write about her, but . . .) moved into a tiny studio apartment in New York, they asked me to help them decorate. I took a train into the city and went with my son to the local home goods store. His girlfriend was overwhelmed at her job and appreciated my help. I felt honored that they asked, but somewhat un-comfortable. As much as I wanted to help my son furnish his very first apartment, I recognized that I did not want to impose on his girlfriend. We were standing in the window treatment section of the store, and my son asked me which curtains I liked. Truthfully, I'm partial to blue but instead I suggested he call his girlfriend at work to ask what color she liked. He did. She liked green. "Perfect," I said. "I love green."

When a son asks a mother her opinion about something that will affect the living quarters of both him and his girl-friend or wife, he's not expecting or looking for any response that could possibly cause a conflict. So you can avoid this by hearing what they—particularly she—have to say first. If they are really undecided and want your help, they'll make that clear. Otherwise, enjoy the fact that they asked, even if it's only out of politeness.

It's a slightly different matter if the young couple asks the boy's mother to buy them a new sofa, but refuses her sugges-tion for color and size. Or asks her to contribute to the cost of the wedding but rejects her opinion as to the time and place. If she's paying, she may feel entitled to weigh in. If that's unac-ceptable, her son and his girlfriend should decline her gift.

Georgia planned a shower for her future daughter-in-law, recommended paint colors for the young couple's new living room, paid for most of the wedding, and then was informed by her new daughter-in-law that she was too controlling. Now, when Georgia makes even a small suggestion ("Don't cut the skin off the peaches. That's where the fiber is!") her daughter-in-law bristles.

The decision to financially help out a couple is unfairly loaded if there are strings attached. All parties need to be aware that how they handle the giving and receiving of monetary gifts can affect the future relationship between the parents and their son and daughter-in-law.

*Woe to the high-spirited bride whose
mother-in-law is still alive.*
     —Congolese proverb

Here Comes the Bride

A woman who dislikes her son's girlfriend can easily keep her feelings to herself, hoping the relationship will eventually dissolve. Then comes the news they're engaged. If the mother had failed to plant the seeds of doubt beforehand, it's unlikely she'll have success now. She'll have little choice but to embrace her son's decision and open her heart and mind to his significant other.

Linda was concerned when her son told her he had become engaged to a charming European woman he had met in graduate school. "The signs that something was wrong appeared a week before the wedding," Linda says. "I kept saying she was nervous. She wouldn't allow the photographers to take a picture before the wedding. She was late for everything; the rehearsal dinner, the shower. It just didn't seem all that important to her."

Still, Linda said nothing to her son. The wedding went off and in fairly short order was followed by a divorce. Like a lot of moms who instinctively know when a wedding is a mistake, the most Linda could hope for was to promise her son support and an open, nonjudgmental reaction if things didn't go as planned. You are not going to stop the wedding. So don't even try. But you can be there with a *stuff like this happens* rather than *I told you so* response for when it doesn't last. The next time he meets someone, as in Linda's case, you will have earned some credibility and a right to inject an opinion.

The truth is, sometimes moms are unhappy initially about the engagement, but as the marriage progresses and their sons seem content, their feelings change. You wouldn't want to have said or done anything to jeopardize that outcome. Amy worried when her son told her he was engaged. She says, "I had hoped that it was for the right reasons. I wasn't going to stop it. I wasn't sure I wanted to. You just close your eyes and jump."

Despite Amy's disappointment, her rocky relationship with her own mother-in-law signaled to her that if she acted less than accepting, she would find herself in the same role with her son's wife. During the wedding planning, she chose "to welcome her in my life, just as I would any of his other friends. My son knows I'm not one of those moms who says, 'You're not good enough for my son.' He's no day at the beach, either!" Because of her efforts to act tolerant and uncomplaining, the wedding planning and actual event went smoothly, and a few months later, Amy and her daughter-in-law found themselves developing a genuine fondness for each other.

Undoubtedly, had Amy created problems before and during the wedding planning, she'd be headed into the same kind of extended silent treatment that she experienced with her own mother-in-law.

Shower Her with Love

If you, as the girlfriend, insist on keeping the boy's control-freak mother out of the wedding planning, then at least allow her to throw you a shower. She can sink her heart and soul, and money, into the event and invite all her friends. And you can grin and bear it.

As the bride-to-be, you deserve to have the day of your dreams—from the wedding gown to the cake and everything that comes in between. But you should appreciate that it's also a day of dreams for all the parents involved. Dole out bits and pieces that you're willing to give up and let them go to town.

When my husband and I were planning our wedding—paid for by my parents, who believed in the tradition of the bride's family paying—my mother opined on every decision, from the site to the music to the food. I tirelessly fought to have things done my way, but two days before the wedding she presented me with a layout of the head table, which was going to include all of my grandparents. She insisted her mother sit next to me (and relegated her mother-in-law to the other end!). It may have been a little odd to see a grandmother next to the bride, but by then I was so worn down I just gave in. Fortunately, it has left me with wonderful memories of my grandmom reaching her fork across to my plate and saying, "Ellie, if you aren't going to eat your carrots . . ."

As a bride, I did get the wedding of my choice. But when it came to the shower, I was happy to leave the details to the moms. A child's wedding is a momentous occasion for a parent, and brides should recognize that. If you don't want to lose control of the big day, then let your future mother-in-law take over one of the preliminary events, such as the shower, rehearsal dinner, or engagement party.

My friend Fran, who has two sons, threw showers for both of her daughters-in-law. She arranged the first party because the young woman's own family wasn't interested in doing so. She planned the second because that young woman's family organized a very small shower that didn't include most of the groom's guests. To the credit of both daughters-in-law, they left the shower exclusively to their future mother-in-law.

If your mother-in-law isn't interested in giving you a shower or acts obligated and not very enthusiastic, then let her off the hook. It's not that she's correct in acting this way—she isn't—but it isn't worth your becoming agitated over her lackluster job. Let someone else plan it, your own family or your bridesmaids, and hope your mother-in-law will at least give you a nice present.

As a bride, years later you'll only remember the wedding reception. So rather than let her overinvolvement in this one part of your wedding bother you, just sit back and enjoy opening your gifts.

Religion Matters

Since weddings are historically steeped in a family's tradition and culture, religious differences often create problems. Even if a couple has satisfactorily resolved their differences, there are bound to be some family members who remain dissatisfied. If religion is important to either the bride's or the groom's parents, compromise in the wedding planning may be required. The couple shouldn't bother, though, with what Aunt Florence thinks.

My parents had wanted Charlie and me to be married by a rabbi in a traditional Jewish wedding. But Charlie wasn't Jewish and, at least in 1975 when we wed, there were few rabbis who would marry an interfaith couple. We conceded to my parents that we would be married by a judge who happened to be Jewish, and Charlie would follow the Jewish tradition of breaking a glass. My in-laws accepted that we were not married in either a church or a synagogue and that Charlie did not convert. It was a compromise that suited all the involved parties, and we ignored the rumblings of any extended relatives on both sides of the aisle.

April, who is Jewish, says her relationship with her son's girlfriend suffered after they became engaged and started to plan the wedding. The bride, who is Catholic, wanted to hold the wedding on a Saturday afternoon so she could more easily accommodate her out-of-town guests. But in Judaism, a wedding cannot be held during the day on a Saturday, the Jewish Sabbath. "It was a major battle, with my son in the middle trying to please his fiancée and his mother," April says. "It was my first tension with his girlfriend." When her son suggested this religious restriction was preventing his fiancée from having the wedding she always dreamed of, April was upset. "I'm all for brides having their dream but also respecting the traditions of the groom's family."

April's son says he and his fiancée had not been concerned about the religious issues until they decided to plan the wedding. "It came out of left field because my mom isn't that religious, but I had to try to explain to my mom that it's my fiancée's day and it's important to me that everything on her wedding day goes the way she wants it."

In the end, the bride's family changed the day to a Sunday, which pleased both April, because it eliminated any religious conflict, and the bride's parents, because the costs were lower. "There was definitely no problem after that," her son says. "The topic just never came back."

A difference in religion often not only disrupts the wedding planning but also puts additional stress on the bride and groom, who want to make both of their families feel comfortable. In the end, someone won't be completely happy. But a bride and groom have to make sure that they have considered their own needs first and then figure out how best to incorporate their families' beliefs. They should address religion and cultural concerns with both sets of parents and find some way to show their respect to all of them. It's always lovely when a bride's or groom's traditional culture is displayed in some way, perhaps through dress, readings, or rituals. It may be the first of countless compromises that—as they will discover—make a marriage strong.

Involving the Mother-in-Law

Clearly, throwing the shower or the rehearsal dinner is not enough for your particular mother-in-law-to-be. She wants to go with you to buy your gown, join you and your mom for the tasting, insist you use her cousin's catering hall, invite friends and neighbors your fiancé has never met. And the cake! She wants it to be layered and traditional with no chocolate accent (because caffeine keeps her awake at night). And you're thinking of multi-tiered cupcakes.

Short of a groom's mother being kept entirely out of the loop, other than to receive an invitation along with everyone else, and without turning over control to her so it becomes her wedding, a bride and groom can and should find a suitable compromise.

If this mom has no daughters, or if this is her first and maybe only wedding of a child, don't deprive her of some of the fun. If you include her in the planning, and she can't keep her mouth shut about the various aspects of the wedding, then figure out how to acknowledge her comments and then make decisions privately with her son. For example, if she envisions your bridesmaids wearing long red gowns, and you're partial to short and peach, tell her this: "That sounds really pretty. I can't wait to run that idea by my bridesmaids. You have such great taste!"

Who knows? Maybe you'll suddenly like red. If not, the next time you speak tell her it was a really tough decision but they're going to wear short and peach. You may then ask her to join you for another aspect in the planning, perhaps the flowers. Florists who deal with weddings will direct their conversations to the bride. The color is already decided by the bridesmaid dresses, and the size is already dictated by the budget.

The choice of venue should be made by you and your fiancé and is obviously determined by the amount of money available. If the groom's parents are paying for the reception, they do get some say. That doesn't mean they decide, but they should be allowed to comment on your choice. If they insist upon nixing it, then say, "Thank you for the money but we'll cover the catering costs ourselves." And be prepared to do just that.

Understandably, the farthest thing from a bride's mind is

how her future mother-in-law is feeling during the wedding planning. I'll tell you. She's feeling lost. She loves this son as much as your mother loves you, but she knows that the role of groom's mother is to speak when spoken to. If you include her now, you will guarantee an easier future together.

I once attended the bridal shower for a friend's daughter, and while I was watching this lovely young woman open her gifts I looked over at the groom's mom. She was sitting by herself, looking a little out of place in a room filled with friends of the bride and the bride's mom. I walked over to her, introduced myself, and told her I imagined it was a little awkward being the mother of the groom. She smiled, and said, "A little bit. But I'm having another shower next weekend for all my friends." Excellent idea.

April understands the discomfort the son's mother might feel during the wedding planning. "I felt very much the mother of the groom through the whole thing." she says. "In the beginning, my son's fiancée said I would be included, but in the end, I wasn't. She had said initially that I would be invited to go dress shopping, and to the caterer's tasting, and then she never asked. I felt hurt."

On the day of the wedding, April wanted the photographer to take pictures of the wedding party before the ceremony. However, the fiancée didn't want the groom to see her. "That didn't sit well with me," says April, who by that day was feeling completely excluded. If she hadn't been left out of the planning, she probably would not have been bothered by the no-photo ruling. If she had been involved from the outset, she would have understood that the bride, whether based on superstition, tradition, or even drama, has every right to decide when the groom can see her.

The person who suffered the most in the wedding planning was April's son. He knew his mother wanted to be involved and he also knew that his fiancée was very close to her own mom.

He says he made a conscious (and correct) decision to put his fiancée's wishes over everyone else's, but he was unhappy that his mother was upset. "I couldn't out-of-sight out-of-mind it," he says.

In other situations, the mother of the groom is more involved in the wedding planning than the mother of the bride, who may not be living or may be estranged from her daughter. Also, if the groom's parents are paying for the wedding, a bride may be happy to work with her mother-in-law-to-be.

Initially, Cindy hadn't been included in her son's wedding planning. Then, sometime after the gown was purchased, the bride had a falling-out with her own mother. Faced with a small wedding paid for by her and her fiancé or a grander one funded by her in-laws, she began including Cindy in the planning. "At that point, it became our wedding. She wasn't talking to her parents. We didn't even know who would walk her down the aisle. So I began to feel, Wow. I never had a daughter but I'm the mother of the bride *and* the groom."

Nicci, too, expects to be involved in planning her son's wedding because she is already very close to his girlfriend. "But I will be cautious," she says "She's the girl and she has a mother. I will take a backseat and wait for them to tell me." The fact is, her son's girlfriend would love for her to be involved. She says, "My boyfriend's mom is hyperorganized and efficient so I would want her involved in the planning as well."

A groom's mom will find that the wedding planning goes smoother if she is careful about when to interject a comment. Not unlike the curtain shopping I did with my son, the mother of the groom should determine the bride's wishes first, even if her opinion is sought. Linda says that when she was asked to pick a color for the bridesmaids, she was careful to say to her future daughter-in-law, " 'What were you thinking?' My daughter-in-law said, 'Blue.' I said, 'Then blue is fine.' "

Not all mothers of grooms want to be involved in the wedding planning. They know it's a tense and difficult period of time and they'd just as soon show up for the party. Meg, for example, who had weddings to throw for her daughters, said she didn't mind not being involved with any of her sons' weddings.

The same was true for Caroline. When her son got married, his girlfriend asked if she would like to join her and her mother in helping plan the wedding. "She asked me to help and I said, 'Tell me what you need and I'll send a check.'" And Sue, who gave her son and his wife some money toward the wedding, allowed the young couple to plan it themselves. They involved her with the caterer and the flowers, which was more than enough for her.

Hope's son actively participated in all aspects of his wedding planning and invited his mom to the tasting, to pick the site, to listen to bands. "When his fiancée went to the fitting, I was invited to see her. But it's not the same as marrying a daughter," says Hope. "Being the groom's mother isn't nearly as much fun as being the bride's mother."

The wedding is clearly an important day in the life of the groom and the bride but, as any married or formerly married couple finds, it's what happens later that really matters.

A few anniversaries from now, no one will remember the color of the flowers.

Money Talks, Someone Walks

Money—who has it, who doesn't, who will offer it, and who refuses—unfortunately drives most weddings. Otherwise, more young couples would elope and forgo their "dream" wedding. Dr. Lazaroff tells of a young couple who were happy together until the money issues surrounding the wedding planning created problems between the two sets of parents.

As soon as they announced their engagement, the guy noticed that his parents acted cold to his fiancée, and her parents became overbearing. "None of this really played out until they got engaged," Lazaroff says. "Once they began planning the wedding, all the dynamics changed. Her parents wanted his family to chip in for the wedding or have the rehearsal dinner at a restaurant. His parents are rather cheap and unsophisticated about etiquette. They wanted to have the rehearsal dinner at their house and were not intending to chip in for the wedding. So it caused a lot of tension between the bride and the new in-laws."

Feelings deteriorated to the point that the bride felt the future in-laws didn't like her, and she began pressuring her fiancé to take control. Meanwhile, her fiancé was criticized by his mother, who insisted he was being overruled. Dr. Lazaroff says, "The man has to identify what he likes and what he wants. He has to talk directly to his parents about finances. In some instances, he agreed his parents were off the wall, and sometimes the fiancée was. My job was to give him the courage to share with his parents how hurt he is about their lack of involvement and interest in the wedding and then how it also hurt his fiancée."

Robert took that step, going with his fiancée directly to her parents. They said they wanted a wedding near their home and for about 350 people, and they would pay for most of it. Robert and his girlfriend wanted a destination affair with a small crowd. Robert told his future in-laws, " 'We can make this so you're happy or so we're happy.' They respected me and followed our wishes."

Even with his taking charge, Robert faced a number of conflicts. His fiancée got upset that the wedding planning was causing an us (her family) against them (his) thing. "She said my mother seemed critical of a lot of the wedding stuff and that was tough because she wanted her approval."

There's no escaping money issues around a wedding, unless—because of a great disparity in incomes—one family graciously decides to pay for everything or neither family pays and the couple picks up the tab. Since most weddings are a combination of everyone taking some role in the finances, hurt feelings are bound to occur. In most cases, once the wedding is long over, these issues will become a fading memory.

The best way to avoid the problems is for the couple to determine their needs and then distribute roles to each family, including additional families created by divorce. It's a little like when a bride registers for her wedding. She has a large wish list, and anyone can purchase from it based on what they can comfortably pay. A close relative might buy that $150 place setting, but a neighbor may go for the $35 wok. If the bride and groom plan every aspect of the wedding and chart the costs involved, they can show the list to their individual parents and see what they are willing and capable of paying for. It doesn't need to be even.

Many of the wedding issues that simmer just below the surface bubble up—or very often erupt—when the invitations are designed. Traditional aspects—one, that the bride's parents pay, and two, that there are only two sets of parents—have gone the way of pillbox hats and the notion that liver is good for you. Today, there are often several contributors to the wedding, including the couple, and any combination of their married, single, divorced, or remarried parents. Yet somehow this one sheet of paper is supposed to reflect all of this.

Marie says she would have preferred that her fiancé's mother had not gotten involved in paying for any part of the wedding. Her own parents paid for the reception and her gown. Her fiancé's dad paid for the honeymoon and then split the rehearsal dinner with her fiancé's mom, even though his parents are divorced. The next morning, the day of the wedding, Marie's fiancé called her to say his mom didn't realize the rehearsal dinner would cost so much; they'd have to cover the check that she gave the restaurant, otherwise it would bounce. "So on our wedding day, we gave *her* a check for a thousand dollars," Marie says. "And she never even gave us a wedding gift."

A Mom by Any Other Name

There was a time not that many years ago when most young brides switched from calling their boyfriend's moms "Mrs. Fisher" to "Mom" once they were married. But today's brides, for many reasons, are very comfortable referring to their mother-in-law by her first name.

Many of these young women have already been in the workforce where they are on the first-name basis with their colleagues, including those old enough to be their parents. Society, in general, is more expectant and accepting of couples living together without being married, and of men and women who get married more than once.

I called my first mother-in-law Mom, but when I remarried in my early forties, it felt a little silly calling my new husband's mother Mom, so I called her by her first name. Ninety percent of the women I interviewed for this book call their mothers-in-law by their first name. And the majority of mothers, even if they would love to be called Mom by their daughters-in-law, will accept whatever they get.

Cindy loves that her daughters-in-law call her Mom, because she feels that "once they marry my son they become my daughter." Maybe it's a reflection of her own situation as a young bride. She says, "The day I got married, I was in the bridal suite and my mother-in-law breezed in. I kept saying, 'Hello, Mother'—I was told to call her that after we got engaged. I'm trying to get her attention. I'm the bride. She was so preoccupied with herself that she ignored me. It was *her* day. She had rhinestones on her eyelashes to match the glitter on her dress. She breezed in. She breezed out. An attendant in the bridal suite said, 'Who was that woman?' I said, 'My mother-in-law.' She said, 'You poor thing.' "

Sue says her daughter-in-law also calls her Mom, though they have a very different relationship from the one she has with her own mother. "She depends on me for clear thought and advice."

On the other hand, Dana calls her new mother-in-law by her first name. She says, "I'm not sure I could ever call her Mom, and frankly, she hasn't asked me to. Actually, when my in-laws refer to each other, they call each other Mr. and Mrs. That's a little weird."

Kelly says her boyfriend's mom would rather she call her by her first name and not by her surname. "I feel weird. I don't think I'll call her Mom when we get married. But I'm most comfortable calling her Mrs. I have to catch myself. I'm close to my mom and my two older sisters. I've already got three moms! I'm not looking for another one. I can take care of myself."

Most mothers-in-law assume their new daughter-in-law can take care of herself, they just want to feel close—like a mom.

———

A wedding is a momentous occasion in the life of the bride and groom as well as in their parents'. It is also a complicated and stressful period with a crush of decisions to be made—both emotional and financial. Everyone is thrown off their best behavior. Don't let this traumatic and exciting time negatively impact the future. What happens after this day is what matters most of all.

Keepsakes

1. When a young couple becomes sexually active, both sets of parents have a responsibility for having "the talk" beforehand.

Don't automatically assume your child was led astray by his or her sexual partner.

2. Sleepovers at his mom's house are the one time she gets to choose when and where. Everyone has to honor that.

3. Excluding your future mother-in-law from all the wedding planning can be unnecessarily hurtful. Pick and choose how best to involve her, but involve her in some significant way.

4. Religious and cultural differences are difficult enough for a young couple to resolve. They need to consider their parents' feelings, but don't allow Uncle Ted or Cousin Renee to weigh in.

5. Money—as in, *who will pay for the wedding?*—opens the door for the parents to comment and influence. A couple must decide together if the outside comments are worth the price.

CHAPTER EIGHT

The Endgame: The Grandkids

Standing in her daughter-in-law's kitchen, her arms protectively wrapped around a velvety blue bundle, Diane had never felt such rhapsody. She drank in the yummy smells of the newborn baby girl, sweet and fragrant like freshly washed laundry airing in the breeze. She lost herself in her eyes, so clear and innocent, and peering back at her, as if to say, *Grandmom, I know you and love you already*. And then . . .

"Don't hold her like that!" screeched her daughter-in-law, shattering Diane's euphoric mood. "Here, give her to me," she said as she took her from her grip and placed her in her infant seat.

It didn't matter that Diane had raised four children of her own, or that she would sacrifice every part of her being for this new child, or that she had purchased the seat that now substituted for her embrace. She stood there and said nothing.

A mother-in-law who has intentionally remained closemouthed during the courtship, the wedding, and the home buying knows that once she becomes a grandmother she will find herself virtually speechless. From the first time she realized her son had fallen in love, her goal has never wavered: to remain a part of her son's adult life and, most important, his offspring's. As a grandmother, she relishes long moments, if not days, of being alone with her grandchild. If she were to create trouble now, she will alienate her daughter-in-law and subsequently, unless she's needed to babysit, will hardly see her grandchildren.

Of course, this doesn't stop some mothers-in-law from offering unwelcome advice to their daughters-in-law, assuming their own experiences as a parent justify their meddling. Cassie's relationship with her mother-in-law changed when complications during her pregnancy kept her off her feet and her mother-in-law came to assist. "We needed her to help with my four-year-old, do the laundry, and make some meals, but she became overbearing. She yelled at me when I got up to go to the bathroom as though I was jeopardizing her unborn grandchild, she fed my daughter sweets like Marshmallow Fluff that I had banned from my cupboards, and she set strict bedtimes not only for my daughter, but for me! After one week, I told my husband she had to go!"

A mother-in-law may want her son and his wife to raise their children in a manner of which she approves, since as far as she's concerned, she's the expert. But some of her ideas are bound to conflict with her daughter-in-law's if for no other reason than that child-rearing recommendations change from generation to generation.

As far as determining what's best for the baby, a new mother is almost always right, having benefited from talking to her pediatrician and to her friends who are also mothers and from reading about the most up-to-date methods for raising children. But often the older mother has something worth saying, aided by experience—both good and bad. The bottom line, however, is that this is the daughter-in-law's turn to raise a child. And the mother-in-law can offer to babysit, buy the stroller, and nod her approval. The sought-after result: an opportunity to spoil her grandchild.

Dying to Ask

Every newly minted mother-in-law has the same question on her mind: *So, have you given any thought as to when you'll have kids?* But many find it a difficult subject to broach with either their son or their daughter-in-law.

If the young couple struggles with infertility, or with an uncertainty as to when or if to have children, a mother-in-law shouldn't impose. This is easier said than done. Not knowing whether she'll become a grandmother is far more frustrating than waiting to find out who her son is taking to his prom. And just like back then, her son could, if he wanted to, put an end to the suspense. At the very least, he could tell his mother whether he and his wife even want children, and if so, whether they would like to start a family immediately or after they are settled in their careers. If the couple keep the mother-in-law entirely out of the loop because they consider the subject highly personal—and understandably so—it can render her a little irrational and nosy beyond necessity.

If you're the daughter-in-law and your husband won't enlighten his mom about your plans to have children, you can relieve her anxiety by giving her a general timeline. "We want to start a family after I'm settled in this job," or "after he finishes graduate school." At some later date, you can fill in the details; for example, "We are working with a fertility specialist," or "We are hoping next Christmas to add another stocking to the mantel."

Linda says, "I used to ask my son when he was going to have kids because he's been married eight years. He said, 'Don't ask me anymore.' I've never asked my daughter-in-law because it's a hard thing to talk to anybody about. I just think they've decided not to tell anyone until and if something happens." Indeed, the prospect of having children is a sensitive subject for her son and his wife; either they disagree on whether to have them or they are having difficulty conceiving. Their reasons are too personal and too emotional to involve a well-meaning but intrusive third party. As frustrating as it is to the son's mother, given her son's obvious reluctance to discuss the topic, she has been left with no choice but to wait it out.

Diane's son and daughter-in-law didn't want anyone to know that they were seeing a fertility specialist. Then one day they needed Diane to drive the young woman to an appointment, so they decided to tell her the truth. The daughter-in-law eventually became pregnant, and then miscarried. That experience was so emotionally devastating that the young couple decided to keep mum about their continuing efforts to conceive. As anxious as Diane was to learn if they had resumed fertility treatments, she knew her asking would be a violation of their privacy. The next time her daughter-in-law became pregnant, she and her husband concealed the news until well into the second trimester.

The issues surrounding a couple's attempts to become pregnant can be uncomfortable to discuss. A young couple deserves the privacy to deal with this issue on their own. If they've been trying unsuccessfully to have children, they do not need to be hounded by one of their parents. I also recognize, however, how anxious the parents are to learn when their son and daughter-in-law plan to have children. This translates into whether they will be around long enough to enjoy them. Melodrama or not, parents all think like this.

So the guy's mother is entitled to ask once: "Do you think you two will have children?"

And the couple should give a suitable response based on their situation at the time. "With any luck, yes" (meaning they are trying), or "Yes, after I get a better-paying job" (they won't try until then), or "No, we don't want children."

That sort of response allows parents to go about their business until—and if—there is news worth sharing.

> *When a child is born, so are grandmothers.*
> —Judith Levy, author

A Crowd in the Delivery Room

Although the mother-in-law should have been involved in the wedding planning, childbirth is an entirely different matter. This time, the mom-to-be gets to choose how much to involve her own mother or her husband's. Everyone has to respect her decision.

Any woman who has been through childbirth knows that those nine months of carrying the baby and the day of delivery are not necessarily up for scrutiny. If I had listened to my superstitious grandmother when I was pregnant with my first child, I wouldn't have raised my arms above my head. (She believed this would cause the umbilical cord to wrap around the baby's neck. Of course, she also believed that cracking an egg over someone's head protected them from influenza.) This event in a woman's life can be as private as she would like, and should never be taken as a reflection of what she thinks of her mother-in-law.

Even if the pregnant woman's own mother shows up in the delivery room, that doesn't mean a mother-in-law will be excluded once the child is born. It's just that in this most intimate moment in a young woman's life, she may feel the need to involve only her significant other, and maybe her mom. So let her.

For the mom-to-be, though, you should remain empathetic to the fact that your mother-in-law is just as excited about your giving birth as is your mother. For both women, this is an extraordinary, profound moment—their child is about to become a parent, and they are about to become grandmothers. So even if you choose to include your mom in the delivery room and not your husband's mom, make sure your mother-in-law gets the first phone call. Insist she come see her new grandchild immediately.

Carol had asked her son and daughter-in-law to call her when labor began so she could meet them at the hospital. But her daughter-in-law refused. "I don't want to run into you when I'm in labor," she told her. A hurt Carol responded, "But I promise, I'll just sit in the waiting room." Her daughter-in-law remained adamant. So Carol waited at home for a phone call, which came within an hour of delivery, and the invitation to come see her new granddaughter, which came a day later.

It was purely by happenstance that Sue ended up in the delivery room with her son and daughter-in-law. She had been having dinner with the young couple and the daughter-in-law's mother when labor started. "Her mom was already intending on being in the delivery room, but I wasn't. Yet when my daughter-in-law went into labor, and I was there, she invited me in."

Sue's daughter-in-law had no obligation to invite her mother-in-law into the delivery room, and even if she included her because it was awkward not to, it was a thoughtful offer on her part. The younger woman acknowledges that her decision was made easier because her mother-in-law had been respectful of her feelings throughout the pregnancy.

That's obviously not the case with all mothers-in-law. Josie says that when she found out she was pregnant with the first grandchild, she couldn't wait to tell all the parents. "My father-in-law was thrilled," she says. "My mother-in-law looked at me and said, 'I'm too young to be a grandmother.' She was annoyed. It interfered with her image of herself."

Showing more self-centeredness, her mother-in-law sched-uled a round-the-world trip for two weeks after Josie's due date. "Then I was late. She said, 'My trip is coming up. You need to ask your doctor to induce this baby.' There was no way I was having this baby at her convenience. It was the first and one of the few times I stood up to her."

Grammy, Bubbie, Grandmom

I grew up calling my father's mother Bubbie, and my mother's mother Grammy. As a child, those names were more identify-ing of my grandmothers than their given names, Fannie Slott and Fay Schultz, which felt oddly strange to me. I just assumed they had always been known as Bubbie and Grammy, and gave little thought to how naming the grandmother is nearly as im-portant as naming the child.

Until, of course, I became a mother, and Charlie and I asked our respective mothers what they would like to be called. Lucky for us, they had different requests. So one became Mommom and one became Grandmom.

My daughter, Debra, was each mother's first grandchild, a very significant occurrence in the naming process. If you beat your siblings to the punch in giving birth to the first grand-child, you will determine what a grandmother will be called. If she already has a name—such as my Bubbie did, since my sister and I were her sixth and eighth grandchildren, respectively—in all likelihood that's the name she'll be called by future grand-kids.

If a grandmother has yet to be titled, then the slate is clean for all sorts of possibilities: Mamma G, Bobo, Oma, Mimzy, Grams, Nan, Toto, Mamma Fisher, Nonna (Italian for "grand-mom"), Ya-Ya (Greek), Abuela (Spanish), Bubbie (Jewish), Granny, Gammie, Gigi, Mimi, G-Ma, G-Mom, and, obviously, Grandma and Grandmom, to name a few.

Since a grandmother's name will remain with her for the rest of her life, and thereafter, she should be allowed to make the final decision. If both mothers want to be called, say, Grandma, then work out a way to personalize them. Maybe make them Grandma-D and Grandma-F for the first initial of their name. In time, your children may end up shortening it to Gran-dee and Gran-fee.

As in Sue's case, many couples bring into a marriage children from a previous relationship. Sue's daughter-in-law had a seven-year-old child, who already had a grandmother he called Grandmom. At first, he struggled with what to call Sue. He tried Mrs. Jones, but when his mom became engaged to Sue's son, that became too impersonal. "My daughter-in-law came up with Sisi, but every time the family got together, her little boy forgot my name. I laughed and said to him, 'We have to decide on a better name.' Once my daughter-in-law became pregnant, my son insisted her son call me whatever the baby would call me. So it's Grandmom Sue. It rolls off his tongue now."

Auntie Em

Although most sisters-in-law will be ecstatic to have a new niece or nephew, occasionally they can feel threatened or envious. Aunt Helen may have been trying to become pregnant herself, or she may see her brother's new baby as usurping the grandparents' attention, or she may worry that her inheritance is becoming diluted.

If you're the sister, you might be critical of the way in which your brother's wife is raising this child, especially if you don't like your sister-in-law. If a grandmother should remain once removed from her grandchild, then you must have one foot out the door. It may be tempting to criticize your sister-in-law's child-rearing talents to your mother, or brother, but it will ultimately come across as petty.

Instead, let it go. Among your brother, his wife, and her parents and yours, there are enough people commenting on the upbringing of this child. So be the fun aunt. It's a great role because it comes with instant adoration from the kids and absolutely no pressure. You're not expected to help pay for college (the grandparents might be). You're not expected to babysit (you have too active a social or professional life). You're not expected to discipline (there's enough of those people).

Be the aunt who calls your nephew or niece directly and offers to take him or her to a movie or skiing or other activity. Attend their games and cheer from the sidelines. Be there for them to talk to as they get to that age when their mother just doesn't get it, but you do.

Sibling rivalry, even if dormant since the preteen years, can easily reappear as Grandmom heaps attention on one grandchild. Paul says his mother has begun spending less time with his wife and more with her other daughter-in-law, who gave birth to the family's first grandchild. Consequently, Paul can't help but feel a little jealous over the amount of attention his nephew receives. His brother and his wife do nothing to discourage these feelings. Whenever Paul tries to visit his new nephew, he's turned away by his brother's wife: "It's not the right time; the baby's sleeping. I'm too tired." Paul's wife doesn't even visit anymore.

Whether intentional or not, a son and his wife can enjoy the attention the grandparents give their child so much so that they don't want to share it with a sibling. Janet says her sister-in-law takes advantage of the control her baby has over the grandparents, despite the fact that Janet has two boys of her own. "My sister-in-law has taken over the family's summer house, telling my husband's parents that if they expect to see their grandchildren, they have to allow them to stay there. That threat is what caused my husband's parents to go along with it. We don't even go to the house anymore."

Since Janet's primary goal is to remain close to her mother-in-law, she can accomplish this despite the fact her sister-in-law is using her own children as pawns. She can encourage her two sons to act appreciative of everything their grandmother does for them. In time, Janet's kids' polite and unpresumptuous side will overshadow the entitled, spoiled actions of her sister-in-law. The contrast, with any luck, will not be lost on the grand-mother.

Out with the Old, In with the New

Diane's daughter-in-law bathed her baby girl, dried her with a soft cotton towel, and put a clean diaper on her. A few minutes later, the baby pooped. Diane watched in horror as her daughter-in-law ignored this new development and put the baby in her high chair. "Why aren't you changing the diaper?" Diane asked.

"Because I'm trying to get her on a schedule," her daughter-in-law responded.

"But newborns go when they have to. They have no schedule."

"Well, she'll have to learn. I only intend to change her diaper every four hours, no sooner and no later," she said. "And when you babysit, you'll do the same. Right?"

Although a mother-in-law might disapprove of some of the ways her grandchild is being raised, she also must recognize that making mistakes is part of child rearing. I turned bedtime into a lengthy ritual when my first child was born. I would feed her, rock her, walk her around, and then wait until she fell asleep in her crib before stealthily leaving her room. When my son was born four years later, I laid him down in his crib. He fussed for a few minutes, and then slept soundly. Today my daughter is a poor sleeper and my son falls asleep instantly. I can't help but think I had a role in their adult nighttime rituals. Obviously, I learned from my mistake as a first-time mother.

Sometimes a grandparent intends to be well-meaning, but her comments can still be aggravating to a new mom. It's the one area Emily says can be difficult to manage with her mother-in-law. "She will put her two cents in and think it's what we need to do to raise our child when my husband and I have other ways of doing it. It can be straining at times. When I listen to her and take her advice, nine times out of ten I wish I had listened to myself and done what I had wanted in the first place. My pediatrician says, 'Your gut maternal instinct is usually right.'"

Amy Goyer, a spokesperson for Grandparents.com, an online resource site for grandparents, says, "Grandparents need to respect the parents' right and ability to make decisions for their kids. And parents need to respect that the grandparents mean well; they love their grandchildren. They all have to have a realistic flexibility."

While this is true, unless a child is physically, emotionally, or verbally abused, a mother-in-law must defer to her daughter-in-law. I'm sure my own mother-in-law questioned some of the ways I raised my kids, but to her credit, she rarely commented. Consequently, I loved to have her babysit my daughter and son, knowing that she would honor my wishes and take very good care of my kids. If she had her own opinions as to how much to feed them and when, or whether they were too young to sit in a restaurant, she kept them to herself.

And if she indulged her grandchildren when I wasn't around, I never knew.

My grandfather used to sneak a "treat" to my sister and me. Two nights a week, he'd come to our house after work. We'd run downstairs to see him just as he was hanging his camel-hair coat in the hall closet. With my mother busy in the kitchen, he'd pull a pack of Life Savers or multicolored Chiclets from his inside coat pocket, hand them to us, and say, "Shhh. Don't tell your mom." Regardless of whether my mom ever found out (I really think she knew all along), the treat signified more than a bit of sugar before dinner; it created a bond between my grandfather and his two grandchildren.

Truthfully, I preferred chocolate, but I adored my Poppa.

It's one thing to relax a son and daughter-in-law's rules—like no candy or bedtime by seven—but it's another to show disregard for the young parents' values. If, for example, your daughter-in-law and son both choose to work full-time and you think one of them should stay home to take care of the children, you need to recognize that this is a decision that works for them and their family. Be respectful—not judgmental.

"I always feel her disdain," Judy says of her mother-in-law, "because I'm a working mother. She always wants to know who will take care of them when they are sick. My husband and I have flexibility with our jobs and one of us can be home by lunchtime. We do what we need to do, and it works for us. We want our kids to know that both parents have successful careers and that they can strive for that, too."

If a grandparent has a serious concern that the child-raising practices of her son and daughter-in-law are damaging to the child, the mother-in-law's first step could be to talk to her son. His response might help her understand the reasoning behind their actions. If he's oblivious to the issue, then she should talk to her daughter-in-law and son together, with sensitivity and without criticism.

Psychologist Lazaroff says, "This should only be about the important things, not the little things. If there is a hostile relationship between the two women, then the mother-in-law's advice will clearly be disregarded. The first thing she should do is mention it constructively to the son so he can pass the tip on to the wife. If he is too passive, then the grandmom herself should very, very gently offer a constructive alternative to the mom's actions so the mom won't be offended." She adds that the two women can't lose sight of the grandchild as the most important person, and that it "often does take a village to raise one."

Cindy refrains from commenting on anything her daughter-in-law does for fear she won't get to be with her granddaughter. Their first disagreement erupted the day the baby came home from the hospital. The new mom believed that if she let her baby sleep in the late afternoon, she wouldn't sleep at night. To ensure that this didn't happen, she began a late-afternoon routine of keeping her awake; she'd talk into her ear, take her clothes off so she'd be cooler and less comfortable, and play with her. It drove Cindy crazy.

"I'm afraid if I say anything to her, she won't let me see my grandchild," says Cindy, who has tried speaking to her son. He, however, defers to his wife on all child-rearing issues. So Cindy no longer intervenes. Unless the child is being mishandled, his own mother and father get to decide what's best for him. The best action for a mother-in-law to take in a situation like this is to make herself invaluable to the couple. Be available to babysit, follow their rules, offer to pick up dinner, food shop, help out with the laundry. A new mother is stressed and exhausted from lack of sleep. If you can be there to help out with items not directly related to the baby, you'll find yourself rewarded with a lot of time with your grandchild.

Remind yourself that every generation revises and personalizes child-raising techniques—just like you did twenty or thirty years ago. If you can accept this, your relationship with your daughter-in-law will flourish. If you can't, everyone will be impacted. I met a woman in the maternity ward when our children—her first, my second—were born. Victoria had every intention of breast-feeding her baby boy. As all new moms know, there is an adjustment period in nursing a newborn. It takes practice and perseverance. When Victoria's very stiff and proper mother-in-law came to visit her new grandson at the hospital, she was aghast to find Victoria trying to nurse.

"Why aren't you giving him a bottle?" she asked her daughter-in-law.

"Because I want to breast-feed him."

Her mother-in-law responded, "That's completely unnecessary," and turned sharply back into the hallway in search of a nurse.

Over the next couple of days while Victoria struggled with learning how to breast-feed, her mother-in-law would enter the room, pick up the baby, and bring him to the nursery where she would get a bottle from an unsuspecting nurse. By the time Victoria packed her bag to go home, it was filled with cans of formula.

Meg insists that she tries not to be like Victoria's mother-in-law and judge the way her daughter-in-law parents, but there are some issues that continue to bother her. "My daughter-in-law says my grandson has a phobia about school and so she homeschools him," Meg explains. "He is smart as a whip yet he won't go to college. He'll be in his twenties and will still be living at home. Her kids raise themselves. There is no set bedtime hour. If they want dinner, she tells them to get a bowl of cereal."

Grandmothers must remember that it is also their sons' responsibility to take part in raising his children. It is too easy for a woman to blame her daughter-in-law and excuse her son, insisting he's either too busy making a living or too powerless to take any action. But mothers-in-law have to analyze honestly whether the issues they have with their daughters-in-law aren't also the fault of their sons. More often than not, the blame should be shared, as should the parenting.

Regardless of the distinct differences between Caroline and her daughter-in-law, she genuinely appreciates that she's included in her grandchildren's lives. And, in fact, her daughter-in-law considers her to be an exemplary grandmother. "One day," Caroline says, "I gathered plastic pans, water, and a beach towel and played with my grandson on the kitchen floor. My daughter-in-law walked in, saw us playing on our imaginary beach, and said, 'I wish I would have known what it was like to have a grandmother like you.'"

Differences aside, there's no better recognition from a daughter-in-law.

Melissa says her relationship with her mother-in-law grew stronger after her first child was born. She babysits whenever they ask and is very involved in their lives. "My mother-in-law and I talk a lot more. She is very helpful and willing to lend a hand whenever she can. Truly, I am so lucky to have her." The key here is that her mother-in-law respects her and her husband's parenting decisions. Melissa adds, "If I ask for advice, she'll give it to me, but she never offers even constructive criticism unless we ask for it."

Religious Differences

As much as religious differences can affect the wedding rituals, they take on an added importance after the birth of the first grandchild. It doesn't matter if the couple were married by both a minister and a rabbi in an effort to appease their families, now comes the real test: Will the child be baptized or circumcised; celebrate Hanukkah or Christmas; join a synagogue or a church? Or will they consider religion a non-issue in raising their children?

Regardless of their decisions, you can be certain the grandparents have an opinion.

Just as the manner of how to potty train or wean off a bottle has been left up to the couple, so should the way in which they embrace religion. They don't need to hear from their parents about what they think; they know it without their saying.

For mothers of sons, up until this point you should have included your son's then-girlfriend, now the mother of his child, in all your religious holidays. If you've excluded her from your

Christmas celebrations because you just wanted to be with your son, then don't expect her to join in now. My mother-in-law smartly included me in her Easter and Christmas holiday events from when I initially dated her son. Nine years later when we had children, I found myself looking forward to going with my family to her warm and welcoming home, and including her in my own celebrations. She introduced me to a Christmas morning breakfast of lox and bagel and eggs and ham, followed by an elaborate opening of dollar stocking stuffers. Today, several years after my mother-in-law's death, my kids and I evoke her memory every Christmas morning. I do just about everything on that holiday the way she did.

As the mother-in-law, use your religious traditions as a way of including your daughter-in-law and not as a way of shutting her out. In the end, you will find yourself sharing your holiday with your grandchildren, regardless of which religion they are being raised.

Amy, who is Jewish, says her Catholic mother-in-law opposed her marriage. Mainly out of love for her husband, but also partly to appease his mother, she agreed to raise their children Catholic. "Both my parents were dead so I didn't have the guilt I may have had otherwise." But because Amy considered this to be a personal sacrifice, when her mother-in-law later blamed her son's marital problems on her, Amy was furious. "I had agreed to raise her grandchildren in her religion, and then when she learned we were having problems, she just assumed it was all my fault. She assumed her son walked on water and I was the bitch of the century." That incident set off the extensive period in which the two women stopped speaking.

If a daughter-in-law decides to raise her children—your grandchildren—in your religion, instead of her own, you must appreciate her considerable and heart-wrenching decision. Do not ever take this for granted. Of course, this works both ways. A daughter-in-law must also appreciate her mother-in-law for acknowledging, and accepting, that her grandchildren are exposed to a different religion.

Sometimes this matters even if the two families are of the same religion but of different intensities. In Caroline's case, both her son and his wife were raised Jewish but over the years his wife became more devout. "When I first met my son's girlfriend, she was an agnostic," Caroline explains. "But shortly before her children were born she became very religious. Now my grandchildren are very much into religion. They go to synagogue with her every Saturday. They speak a lot of Hebrew in the house. One time, my grandson said he wanted to teach me Hebrew. I said, 'I don't want to learn Hebrew.' He said, 'But Grandmom, Hebrew is important.' I said, 'Not to me. And I don't want to learn it.' I'm going to be honest with him because I want him to learn who I am."

Still, Caroline says she honors the way her daughter-in-law has chosen to raise her children, and when they visit her she is very respectful of following the same sort of practices they do at home. Everyone wins. Her son and daughter-in-law happily spend time at Caroline's, and the grandchildren look forward to visiting Grandmom.

> *When grandparents enter the door,*
> *discipline flies out the window*
> —Ogden Nash, poet

Discipline: Spare the Rod

You believe in sending your child to bed without supper because he refuses to eat his peas. She believes in making two dinners so the children don't have to eat something they don't like. You think a child should be grounded for a month for disobeying curfew. She thinks depriving him of watching his favorite television show is enough of a punishment.

What happens when the mother-in-law and daughter-in-law disagree on the way to discipline a child, whether it's a toddler experiencing the terrible twos or a teenager entering his rebellious period?

According to grandparenting expert Amy Goyer, "Of all the many things they fight about, discipline is a big one. Maybe at Grandmom's house a grandchild is allowed to do something that at home he or she isn't, or vice versa. Everyone has to communicate about what's going on and be willing to compromise. People, though, get caught up in their own selfishness and they are not thinking about the child."

I would go a step further and say that if there is no compromise, the final decision rests with the child's parents. A grandparent will undermine the effectiveness of a lesson learned if they openly disagree with their son and daughter-in-law's form of discipline—so long as it falls within the parameters of acceptable parenting.

Dr. Lazaroff also stresses that discipline is primarily the parents' responsibility. She says, "If one or both parents are around, the grandmother should not take on the disciplinary role. However, if she is alone with the child for whatever reason, then as a responsible adult she should try to protect and teach the child what is right. It is okay for her to put the child in a time-out if necessary. She can also reward the child for excellent behavior. The point here is that as a loving member of the child's family, she has a right and a duty to help the child in a constructive manner. Grandparents can be a wonderful resource of strength and wisdom for a child, and this resource should be valued."

Early on, the parents should identify the grandparent's role in the areas of discipline and in conferring with teachers, doctors, babysitters, and other professionals in the grandchild's life.

Caroline intervened with her grandson's teacher one afternoon when she went to pick him up from school, but her daughter-in-law, who is usually very appreciative of all Caroline does, was livid. "All I did was suggest to his teacher that he sit in the front of the room because he has a hard time staying focused." Her daughter-in-law "went bonkers." Caroline says, "She was angry that I had said anything to the teacher."

Does a grandmother have a right to speak to her grandchild's teacher or coach or babysitter without the expressed consent of both parents? No. It's important for all of us mothers (mother-in-laws or daughters-in-law) to have the proper perspective on this. As much as I would want to speak directly to my grandchild's teacher if I were concerned about something and the opportunity presented itself, I would have no right to do so without my son *and* daughter-in-law's permission. When I was a young mother, I would have been vexed at my mother-in-law, and my own mother, for that matter, if they'd interceded without my asking. Grandmothers don't always have the entire picture. The parents may have been working with the child's behavioral issue and feel he is showing some progress, or they know that this particular teacher will be more difficult on their child if she is privy to certain information, or they know the other kids on the team will torment the child if someone speaks to a coach on his behalf. It has to be their decision. But that doesn't mean a grandmother can't ask permission.

Now, if a grandparent is given more authority with the grandchildren—perhaps she is their prime caregiver during the day when both parents are working—she may find herself in a situation of being better able to address certain issues. In that case, she should still speak to the child's parents first. They may welcome her involvement and encourage her, for example, to speak to their son's math tutor.

With behavioral issues, a grandmother may feel a more pressing need to address the problem. And she may find herself at odds with her daughter-in-law. She has to know when to re-main silent and when to interject. Obviously, if the child's be-havior is destructive to himself or to others, a grandmother has every right to intervene.

The right to discipline becomes even more clouded when the grandchild is the daughter-in-law's child from a prior mar-riage, as in Sue's case. Her son is raising the seven-year-old son from his wife's first marriage and so Sue spends as much time with him as she does with their new baby.

"When they first got married, she'd bring her son. He was very active, usually eats on the run. I'm more of a disciplinarian than my daughter-in-law is. I'd make my kid sit at a table." Sue decided to handle the situation by disciplining her step-grandson only when he was in her house. "If I am at my son and daughter-in-law's house, I say nothing. When he's at my house, I say, 'You don't jump on the furniture. You wash your hands before eating. Sit down at the table.' To my daughter-in-law's credit, she backs me up when I discipline. She'll say, 'Listen to Grandmom.'"

According to Dr. Lazaroff, "If a child is a step-grandchild, the grandmother has to first ask her son and daughter-in-law to define her role. Is she just an older friend or is she one of the grandmothers? If she is viewed as a grandmother, then the same rules apply as with all grandparents. If she is just an older friend, then she should step in responsibly if she is the only adult with the child. This is a sticky one because the mother of the child may not even allow the stepdad to discipline in any way. So the way the roles are explained will make a difference."

It's important that when there is a grandchild from a prior marriage, the grandmother use the same form of discipline for that child as well as for any children born to her son and his wife. This is a wonderful opportunity to get close to your daughter-in-law's children, and that will go a long way toward helping you get close to her. And you all know where that leads.

Grandkids as Leverage

Although Caroline and her daughter-in-law recognize there are distinct differences between them and how they would raise the children, Caroline says she has never worried that the differences could result in her not seeing her grandchildren. "I don't think if we had a fight, she would use the children as weapons."

But in many families, as evidenced by the number of emails received by AARP and Grandparents.com, Amy Goyer says, when a mother-in-law doesn't get along with her son's significant other, that's exactly what happens.

Michele, still stewing over her in-laws' decision not to contribute to her wedding, and tired of her mother-in-law's antics throughout her courtship, has cut off all communication with them. Her husband agrees with her. Throughout her pregnancy, she refused to speak to them. Since her child was born, she has denied them an opportunity to see their first grandchild.

"There are so many grandparents in this situation and they feel so helpless," says Goyer, adding that most states have laws that allow grandparents to petition the court for visitation rights. Grandparents are more likely to have success if the situation involves a non-intact family; meaning one in which there has been a divorce or the death of a parent. But generally, if the parents are married, as in Michele's case, the courts favor the parents.

Goyer says a grandparent could hire an attorney or consider mediation, which she says "is always going to be a better option."

"If the parents agree to mediation, you're there," adds prominent family law attorney Cheryl Young. "Maybe they are willing to allow visitation but they just couldn't come up with a suitable agreement. Then mediation can be helpful. But if the couple is in an intact marriage, and they don't want to let the grandparents see the kids, the grandparents aren't going to be able to do anything. If they are in a happy marriage, they can cut off the grandparents and the court is not going to let a third party to come in. You have to have a family that is already broken to allow custody."

There are circumstances that improve a grandparent's chance of receiving visitation rights. For example, in a typical divorce both the mom and the dad have time with the children, and therefore, presumably the grandparents can see their grandchildren when they are with their child. But if one of the parents is dead, or one is in prison, or a father, for example, relinquished his rights after being accused of abusing the mom and so she has sole custody, a grandparent has a greater opportunity to be involved. It always has to be in the best interest of the child.

"I think grandparents are well aware of their rights," says Young. "They are a pretty vocal group. They love their grandkids and they don't want to be cut out." Involved means visitation only. It doesn't mean legal custody to have a say in important child-rearing decisions such as what religion to raise the kids, or what school to go to. "They aren't going to get that. That is very rare."

Grandparents can find information from the AARP Foundation (www.aarp.org/grandparents); the American Bar Association (www.abanet.org/family/familylaw/tables.html), which lists the visitation laws in each state; Elderlaw Hotlines (www.aoa.gov/eldfam/Elder_Rights/Legal_Assistance/Legal_Hotline.asp); Grandparents.com (www.grandparents.com); and a mediation hotline (www.mediate.com).

"There are some grandparents who are a mess and shouldn't see their grandkids," Goyer says, "but the bottom line is you have to do what is right for the child."

Marie has little patience for her mother-in-law, and even less respect for how she would raise a child today. She no longer engages her; instead she leaves any communication with her up to her husband. "He does all the fighting for us now," Marie says. The one hook they have is her grandson. "She will call and ask if she can come over," Marie says. "Sometimes I say 'Yes,' sometimes 'No. It's not a good time.' She knows she has to be careful." Marie insists that her mother-in-law is only interested in being around her grandchild if she has an ulterior motive. "My daughter is a prop for her. She lives fifteen minutes from her grandchildren and only calls to see them if there is someone around she wants to show them off to."

Marie also believes she can't leave her children alone with her mother-in-law because she's convinced her husband's mom would be so scatterbrained that she would let them fall off the top of a jungle gym and say, "Woe is me." In reality, sometimes a daughter-in-law has a genuine concern about her aging mother-in-law's ability to tend to her grandchildren. In these situations, rather than leave your child alone with his grandmother, plan events and activities that include everyone. You can keep a watchful eye.

Children benefit from having grandparents in several ways: Their confidence is strengthened because there is someone else who loves them unconditionally; they grow up with an appreciation for the elderly; they learn how to communicate across generational lines; they can learn from someone who actually experienced Woodstock, Nixon's resignation, and the explosive growth of technology.

"Everyone knows," Goyer adds, "that the more caring adults a child has in his life, the better he will do."

It really does take a village.

———

As a mother-in-law you should be available, but not interfering, and respectful of your daughter-in-law's parenting style. You should recall how you felt as a new mom when your own mother-in-law questioned your introduction of solid foods and your method of potty training.

As a daughter-in-law you should be tolerant of your mother-in-law's excessive worry over her grandchild. In this vast world, few people will ever come close to loving and caring for your child the way you do. One of those people is your mother-in-law.

It may help to remember that one day you may have a son. And he'll have a girlfriend.

Keepsakes

1. Moms must recognize that a young couple's decision to start a family is personal and private. Ask once but do not bombard your son and his wife with questions.
2. Dr. Spock was so last century. Understand that child-raising techniques change over time.
3. Grandparents do not assume the role of parent—whether in regard to discipline or addressing teachers and coaches—unless expressly asked to do so by their son and his wife.
4. Rather than tell his mother what you want the grandchildren to call her, ask her what she would prefer.
5. A woman you view as a difficult mother-in-law may very well be viewed by your children as a loving grandmom. And that is something for which to be truly grateful.

Epilogue

If one thing has remained constant in the writing of this book it's that, for better or for worse, change is inevitable. Some of the moms and their sons' significant others have become closer, while others no longer speak. What is clear is that this is a two-way street. In fact, once you consider the extended family and the son himself, it's a traffic jam: There is no movement, unless someone gives.

What follows is an update on some of the men and women who've allowed us to peek into their lives.

———

First, the moms:

Lily, who at one point thought her son's high school sweetheart would just fade away, realizes now that she isn't going to. And Lily is fine with that. The young couple moved in together, and they both appear to be happy and very much in love. Accepting this development, Lily has begun spending more time with her son's girlfriend, and the two women have "grown much closer."

———

Amy regrets that her instincts were right. She had been irked by her son's girlfriend for repeatedly breaking up and getting back with him, and for acting rude during their family Christmas celebration. But once the young woman became her daughter-in-law, Amy was determined to forget the past. The wedding was wonderful and served as the occasion for Amy to renew a loving relationship with her mother-in-law and sister-in-law, with whom she hadn't spoken in a decade. Although Amy's good relationship with her husband's family continues, her son's happiness was short-lived. Less than a year after the wedding, he announced he and his wife were getting divorced.

———

Jill's son's needy girlfriend remains in his life, and he still confides in his mother. "When he starts complaining, I always answer the same, 'She's not the problem. You are. You cannot change people. If you don't like her, you have to leave. She never will.' I stay out of it until asked, but it's not easy. He and I are able to talk so he harbors no resentment toward me."

———

Nicci's son's girlfriend is now her daughter-in-law. They were close before, and she says they continue to be. Planning the wedding was a lot of fun because her son and daughter-in-law involved both sets of parents in the decision making (they shared the expenses) and everyone has been getting along.

———

April continues to worry about her son's wife and her dependence on her own parents, but she's learned to accept that this is whom her son has picked. "The things I love about my daughter-in-law I still do, and the things I don't like about her I still don't like. However, I think my attitude has changed. I realize I need to relate to the daughter-in-law I have, not the one I want her to be. I tell myself that the secret to being happy in life is to lower your expectations of people, and you won't be disappointed. This seems to help."

Cindy says that although she may disagree with some aspects in how her daughter-in-law parents, she believes that they've come to an understanding. By Cindy limiting her comments to only her major concerns, her daughter-in-law is more receptive to suggestions about child rearing, and Cindy is more tolerant when they're not followed. "I have a newfound admiration for many of her parenting skills. She never raises her voice or loses her temper no matter how trying my grandchild's behavior might be," Cindy says. "I know that no matter what happens, she and my son will always consider me a vital part of my granddaughter's life."

Caroline may still disagree with much of the way her daughter-in-law raises her children, but the two women get along very well, and the grandchildren spend a lot of time at Caroline's. She always makes a point of honoring their dietary needs and religious observances when they come to visit, and then resumes her own customs once they leave.

And the girlfriends and wives:

Marie's relationship with her hippyish mother-in-law hasn't changed, but her husband's has. The mom had gone to Florida to recover from a shoulder problem and didn't call for weeks. In the interim, Marie's father-in-law, who is divorced from the mom and has a serious girlfriend, invited Marie and her husband to Easter dinner. When his mom came home a few days

before the holidays, Marie says she became enraged upon learning they were planning Easter with her ex-husband. "At that
point, my husband said 'Enough is enough.' We now only meet
up for outings on neutral territory; a restaurant, museum, or
kids' concert. While I feel that my children are missing out on a
true grandmother experience, I feel this is the only way we can
all get along. My children do enjoy time with her, but she's only
good for about ninety minutes and then she 'has to be somewhere.' The great thing is that my father-in-law and his girlfriend are terrific with the kids. Now I just need to make sure
they stay together!"

———

Kelly says her boyfriend's mom is much friendlier when they
see each other, but unless Kelly makes an effort to speak on the
phone or to arrange an outing, they do not communicate. Interestingly, her boyfriend holds a different view. He says his
mother has "embraced Kelly" and is even bugging him to marry
her.

———

Hannah was heartbroken when her romance with Vijay broke
off because of his interfering mother, who didn't want her son
to date someone of a different culture. But Hannah says that
was a "blessing in disguise," because she has since become engaged to another man, who also happens to be from another
culture and religion. "Even though his mother and I haven't
met face-to-face (she lives in Jordan), we've spoken several
times through his webcam and she tells my fiancé that she already loves me." Now it's Hannah's parents who are worried
their daughter will face challenges in an interfaith marriage.
But Hannah is extremely happy, saying that her fiancé is completely accepting of their differences, and they can't wait to get
married. By the way, Vijay, who knows about her engagement,

has asked to meet for a cup of coffee. Hannah keeps putting him off, knowing she has no desire to see him—or his mother—ever again. "I've concluded that he never really wanted to marry me, or he would have gone against his mother's wishes."

———

Jenny says that ever since her boyfriend had a heart-to-heart with his mom and his sister, everything has changed for the better. So much so that Jenny is now "welcomed with open arms into the family. It's been a big difference and I am really happy about it!"

———

When Melissa developed a severe eye infection late one night, her mother-in-law rushed over and took her to the hospital so her husband could stay home with their six-month-old baby. "My mother-in-law didn't complain, wasn't upset, and actually insisted that she come help us out. I feel very lucky to have her."

———

Nonnie has since married her boyfriend, and her relationship with her mother-in-law remains strong. However, her some-what strained relationship with her own mother intensified during the wedding planning. "If not for my husband, my mother and I would be in a really bad place. He really func-tioned as an intermediary between us. In the weeks before the wedding, all wedding-related communication from my mom went straight to him and it helped to keep me sane."

———

On the day of her wedding, Emily became overwhelmed when the bridal room started filling up with friends and family. "I just wanted to be by myself and reflect for a minute or two," Emily says. "My mother-in-law saw this and immediately took me outside for a breath of fresh air, away from all those people. She also got me a glass of wine. What a relief! It was just what I needed and she just knew. I can't ask for a better mother-in-law."

———

And some of the sisters:

Sharon says for a long time her brother would visit without his wife, making excuses for her: She had a fear of flying, or she had conflicting plans. When the entire extended family went on a cruise, the sister-in-law stayed home claiming motion sickness. Then one of her other brother's children graduated from college, and the sister-in-law joined the family for the first time in years. "When we found ourselves sitting next to each other, we talked. She knew very little about my life, as if my brother never discussed me with her. I had had surgery a few months earlier, which she knew, but had no idea what kind of surgery." It occurred to Sharon that her brother has some culpability in helping to create the distance between the two women. As a result, she is beginning to feel less animosity toward her sister-in-law.

———

Nothing has changed in Janet's relationship with her sisters-in-law. She continues to have a good relationship with her mother-in-law even though she clearly comes last, behind the daughters. Fortunately, though, her husband now recognizes the inequality and completely supports his wife. Unfortunately, he's yet to say anything to either his mother or his sisters.

———

Laura says her brother is dating the "psycho" girlfriend and remains indecisive about the relationship. "He opens up to me about it, but I am all out of advice so I just listen and tell him we have had this conversation a million times." She believes she'd probably like a different girlfriend.

———

With the realization that her brother's girlfriend will very likely become her sister-in-law, Candace has started over with developing a relationship with the other woman. For the first time in the couple's lengthy romance, Candace and her brother's girlfriend have reached out to each other. They have become much closer and are actually becoming friends.

———

And some of the guys:

Paul says his mom and his wife have developed a "kind and compassionate relationship and are both supportive of each other when either is in need." He believes that since he married Jess nearly two years ago, the two women have become closer. But this didn't happen without Paul's intervention. He confronted his mom, accusing her of befriending her other daughter-in-law to the exclusion of Jess. "They are both really treated equally now and my mom sees them both as wonderful daughters-in-law."

———

William has made a significant discovery. "Things are great with my mom and my sisters actually, much improved," he says. "Ironically enough, I realized I was a lot of the problem. All I really had to do was show excitement about Nina to my mom and sisters rather than hiding her and separating our relationship from them. They've all been great to her recently and I think she feels a lot more welcomed in my family."

———

Adam and Allie have broken up. No matter how he spins it, he says his mother had a lot to do with it. "It was really more my immaturity and my feeling that there is so much I want to do in life before I settle down, but I would be remiss if I said that my mom had nothing to do with it. She was definitely a factor."

———

Joe says he has witnessed a change in how his mother reacts to his girlfriend, and it's for the better. "She even asks me uncomfortable questions about when I plan on proposing." However, Joe admits that his mother and his girlfriend rarely see each other, so that his assessment as to why his mom has become more accepting is probably just the result of time and of the fact that his mom doesn't particularly like his brother's girlfriend. Regardless, Joe finds that life is easier when his mother and his girlfriend seem to get along.

———

Robert is now happily married. He told his mother-in-law and his mother that the relationship between him and his wife took precedence to anyone else's concerns. Neither his mother nor his mother-in-law comes first in their relationship, and everyone is finding a way to respect that. Way to go, Robert!

———

And finally, that brings me to my son. He and the girlfriend I mentioned in the introduction are currently living in different cities. If they should get back together or if he should find someone new, I know I will welcome any woman with open arms. It's not a question of "It's Either Her or Me," but rather her and my son, and then me.

I wouldn't have it any other way.

ELLIE SLOTT FISHER is the author of the critically acclaimed *Dating for Dads* and *Mom, There's a Man in the Kitchen and He's Wearing Your Robe*. A long-time journalist and relationship expert, Fisher has been featured in numerous magazines as well as the anthology, *Single Woman of a Certain Age*. Fisher lives outside Philadelphia. Her website is Elliefisher.com.